EARTHQUAKES PROPHESIED

EARTHQUAKES PROPHESIED

STANLEY
HOERMAN

BOB
ARMSTRONG

CREATION
HOUSE

Earthquakes Prophesied: Beware!
By Stanley Hoerman and Bob Armstrong
Published by Creation House
A Charisma Media Company
600 Rinehart Road
Lake Mary, Florida 32746
www.charismamedia.com

Design Director: Justin Evans
Cover design by Lisa McClure

Address all correspondence to:
Stanley Hoerman
Earthquake
P. O. Box 988
Manhattan, KS 66505
Or bobkimandb@gmail.com

Library of Congress Cataloging-in-Publication Data: 2015939484
International Standard Book Number: PB: 978-1-62998-457-5 / HB: 978-1-62998-459-9
E-book International Standard Book Number: 978-1-62998- 458-2

First edition

15 16 17 18 19—987654321
Printed in Canada

DISCLAIMER

THE INFORMATION PROVIDED in this book is without warranty of any kind and, in particular, no representation or warranty, expressed or implied, is made nor is to be inferred as to the accuracy, timeliness, or completeness of any such information. Under no circumstances shall Stanley Hoerman, Bob Armstrong, or any ministries they are associated with have any liability to any person or entity for a loss or damage in whole or in part caused by, resulting from, or relating to any error (neglect or otherwise) or other circumstances involved in procuring, collecting, compiling, interpreting, analyzing, editing, transcribing, transmitting, communicating, or delivering such information, or any direct, indirect, special, consequential, or incidental damages whatsoever.

This book is for displaying our opinions only and does not necessarily reflect the views of any ministries we are involved in. Any news or links are the subject matter of those sources and not necessarily the opinion of the authors. All statements herein are made without prejudice and malice. Statements about future events are made from researched documents and do not constitute any liability or malice if these events do not occur.

This book is dedicated to my lovely wife Rose Marie. She has encouraged me as the Lord showed me to write this book. She has not only helped so many people along her life's journey, but has also served for many years in the leadership of the Manhattan, Kansas, Women's Aglow organization. She was state leader of Northeast Kansas for Women's Aglow.

—**Stan Hoerman**

This book is dedicated to my wife of over three decades, Kim. Thank you for standing with me, through thick and thin, and always encouraging me. You have always pointed me to our God and His greatness. This has caused my compass for life to always be abundantly fulfilled.

Also, this book is dedicated to all the fearless prophets and those who diligently study prophecy, who have stepped out in faith throughout the ages, who have been ridiculed by the world and the secular news media. Praise God for your faithfulness.

—**Bob Armstrong**

FOREWORD

I HAVE READ EARTHQUAKES *Prophesied.* I believe it is of importance to many of today's Christians because we know little of their significance.

Earthquakes have our attention all the time, especially those of us that live on the west coast of North America. The authors have compiled a treatise on how they happen, their form, and their frequency around the world. Our Holy Scriptures make many references to their occurrence during biblical times. It is quite apparent that the Lord attaches great significance to their effect on humanity and employs them to attract our attention. Christ's death and resurrection from Earth 2000 years ago were both marked with a great quake.

Many thoughtful men of the Bible today are drawing our attention to them in current and future events. We should take note of their pronouncements, but unfortunately, most of us are unaware of these prophecies. In this review, we are directed to many of their visions, dreams, and thoughts regarding our present times. A map is presented of the United States indicating many diverse areas: east and west coastal areas, intermountain states, Texas, Florida, and the Madrid fault quake area in the central United States.

Jesus said there will be quakes in various areas. The government agencies of the United States and the United Kingdom state earthquakes are not more frequent today than the past. We are puzzled! How can this be? Are the final days close? However, many people you speak with feel they are more frequent. One of the many experts in this review gives a clue as to how this is possible.

—WAYNE A. GEYER, PROFESSOR OF FORESTRY
KANSAS STATE UNIVERSITY

CONTENTS

PREFACE

MUCH OF THE critical information within this book is a compilation of writings by various prophets who believe that earthquakes are a definitive sign of the end-time days on this earth.

We realize that the title of this book *Earthquakes Prophesied: Beware!* may seem quite disconcerting to the normal reader. We promise you, we are not "alarmists," and we are not "end-time conspiracy" nuts. But we do read the Word of God, and we do listen to and read legitimate prophets.

There's a reason why we say "legitimate" prophets. The prophetic times have gone onto the fast track. Even though most churches do not teach much about prophecy, there is a great interest in the times in which we live and how they relate to the future, according to the Bible.

However, with increased interest in prophecy and how our times are influenced by it, there have appeared out of the woodwork many false prophets who give supposed prophecies for their own financial gain. Most claim to be Christian, yet they are rewriting the Scriptures for their own purposes by interjecting their own interpretations. Many Bible verses are taken out of context to be manipulated by these false prophets.

Often opinions are taught as fact, and many people cannot accurately sort fact from fiction. One must always ask, "Does this prophecy line up with the Holy Bible?" That is the ultimate test. Many false prophets herald their personal opinions with this statement: "I know the Bible says this, but the Holy Spirit is telling me this!"

But what does the Bible say about the false prophets? "See to it that no one misleads you" (Matt. 24:4, NAS). Another version says, "Take heed that no man deceive you" (KJV).

Peter warned of false prophets in 2 Peter 1:21—2:3:

> For no prophecy was ever made by an act of human will, but men moved by the Holy Spirit spoke from God.
>
> But false prophets also arose among the people, just as there will also be false teachers among you, who will secretly introduce destructive heresies, even denying the Master who bought them, bringing swift destruction upon themselves. Many will follow their sensuality, and because of them the way of the truth will be maligned; and in their greed they will exploit you with false words; their judgment from long ago is not idle, and their destruction is not asleep.

False prophets get in over their head with what we call extra-biblical, self-indulgent, or emotional prophecies.

The Bible speaks of these purveyors of prophecies that are twisted for their own purposes.

> For the time will come when they will not endure sound doctrine; but wanting to have their ears tickled, they will accumulate for themselves teachers in accordance to their own desires, and will turn away their ears from the truth and will turn aside to myths. But you, be sober in all things, endure hardship, do the work of an evangelist, fulfill your ministry.
>
> —2 TIMOTHY 4:3–5

The Holy Spirit will not direct you to depart from the precise Word of God. That's what we adhere to in this book. Prophecies given in this book are from proven, well-known, and godly prophets and prophetesses. What we pray you will learn from this book is that God speaks through His servants, the prophets. Many people will not accept them as prophets until what they say comes to pass. By the time the events take place, it is too late to get the word out or do anything about it.

Before we put this book together, we only knew about Mother Shipton, William Branham, and Jim Bakker. Many people will believe what is on the Internet and not the Bible. How can so many people through the years have such detailed description of what will happen decades in advance? Read and decide for yourself.

Momentarily, forget about the prophets, and read what the Bible says about the future. Dwell on these important end-time Scriptures as you think about the earthquakes that are surely coming. Here are some verses to contemplate.

> My people are destroyed for lack of knowledge.
> Because you have rejected knowledge,
> I also will reject you from being My priest.
> Since you have forgotten the law of your God,
> I also will forget your children.
>
> —Hosea 4:6

> "You only have I chosen among all the families of the earth; therefore, I will punish you for all your iniquities."
> Do two men walk together unless they have made an appointment?
> Does a lion roar in the forest when he has no prey?

Does a young lion growl from his den unless he has
captured something?
Does a bird fall into a trap on the ground when
there is no bait in it?
Does a trap spring up from the earth when it
captures nothing at all?
If a trumpet is blown in a city, will not the people
tremble?
If a calamity occurs in a city has not the LORD
done it?
Surely the Lord GOD does nothing unless *He reveals
His secret counsel to His servants the prophets.*
A lion has roared! Who will not fear?
The Lord GOD has spoken! Who can but prophesy?"

—AMOS 3:2–8, EMPHASIS OURS

I looked when He broke the sixth seal, and there was *a great earthquake;* and the sun became black as sackcloth made of hair, and the whole moon became like blood; and the stars of the sky fell to the earth, as a fig tree casts its unripe figs when shaken by a great wind. The sky was split apart like a scroll when it is rolled up; and every mountain and island were moved out of their places. Then the kings of the earth and the great men and the commanders and the rich and the strong and every slave and free man hid themselves in the caves and among the rocks of the mountains; and they said to the mountains and to the rocks, "Fall on us and hide us from the presence of Him who sits on the throne, and from the wrath of the Lamb; for the great day of their wrath has come; and who is able to stand?"

—REVELATION 6:12–17

For nation will rise against nation, and kingdom against kingdom, and in various places there will be famines and *earthquakes.*

—Matthew 24:7, Emphasis Ours

There will be *great earthquakes,* and in various places plagues and famines; and there will be terrors and great signs from heaven.

—Luke 21:11, Emphasis Ours

And the temple of God which is in heaven was opened; and the ark of His covenant appeared in His temple, and there were flashes of lightning and sounds and peals of thunder and an *earthquake* and a great hailstorm.

—Revelation 11:19

INTRODUCTION

NOW IS THE time when there will be sorrow in the world that no human comfort can heal. The Spirit of God is being retracted. Disasters by the sea and by land follow one another in quick succession. How repeatedly we hear of earthquakes and tornadoes; of destruction by flood, fire, and explosions—with great loss of life and property. These disasters are unpredictable outbreaks of disorganized, unregulated forces of nature, wholly beyond the control of man—but in them all, God's purpose may be read. They are among the agencies by which He seeks to awaken men and women to a sense of their danger.

What exactly is an earthquake? An earthquake is considered a "seismic event" that generates seismic waves. Most of us understand the word from the television reports that mention the "epicenter." This is the ground level point that is directly above the hypocenter, which is the initial rupture point underground. We recognize earthquakes as a shift of the ground which causes tremors or a literal shaking of the earth. As a result, sometimes volcanoes or landslides can occur, in addition to massive destruction of property and sometimes human lives.

If an earthquake happens offshore, many times a tsunami effect is caused, creating violent flooding.

Wikipedia defines an earthquake in this way:

> An earthquake (also known as a quake, tremor or temblor) is… [the] result [of a] sudden release of energy in the Earth's crust that creates seismic waves. The seismicity, seismism or seismic activity of an area refers to the frequency, type and size of earthquakes experienced over a period of time.
>
> Earthquakes are measured using observations from seismometers. The moment magnitude is the most common scale on which earthquakes larger than approximately 5 are reported for the entire globe. The more numerous earthquakes smaller than magnitude 5 reported by national seismological observatories are measured mostly on the local magnitude scale, also referred to as the Richter magnitude scale.
>
> These two scales are numerically similar over their range of validity. Magnitude 3 or lower earthquakes are mostly almost imperceptible or weak and magnitude 7 and over potentially causes serious damage over larger areas, depending on their depth. The largest earthquakes in historic times have been of magnitude slightly over 9, although there is no limit to the possible magnitude. The most recent large earthquake of magnitude 9.0 or larger was a 9.0 magnitude earthquake in Japan in 2011 (as of March 2014), and it was the largest Japanese earthquake since records began. Intensity of shaking is measured on the modified Mercalli scale. The shallower an earthquake, the more damage to structures it causes, all else being equal.[1]

Southern California receives much of the attention of earthquakes. According to the United States Geographical Society,

> Every year, there are over 10,000 earthquakes in southern California. Most of them are so small that they are not felt. Only several hundred are greater than magnitude 3.0, and only about 15-20 are greater than magnitude 4.0. If there is a large earthquake, however, the aftershock sequence will produce many more earthquakes of all magnitudes for many months.[2]

Earthquakes are a very definitive part of the Holy Scriptures:

> Now as He sat on the Mount of Olives, the disciples came to Him privately, saying, "Tell us, when will these things be? And what will be the sign of Your coming, and of the end of the age?" Jesus answered and said to them.... "And there will be... earthquakes in various [diverse] places."
>
> —Matthew 24:3–7, nkjv

> When you see these things happening, know that it is near—at the doors!
>
> —Mark 13:29, nkjv

As we have already read, the Bible talks about "earthquakes in diverse places." God has used earthquakes in numerous ways and for diverse reasons throughout history. By the same token, He will use earthquakes and prophetic events to help herald the return of Christ to this earth.

Earthquakes are more commonplace today than ever before in the history of civilization. As we draw closer to His soon return, there will be more earthquakes.

> For nation will rise against nation, and kingdom against kingdom. And there will be earthquakes in

> various places, and there will be famines and troubles. These are the beginnings of sorrows.
>
> —MARK 13:8, NKJV

> And there will be great earthquakes in various places, and famines and pestilences; and there will be fearful sights and great signs from heaven.
>
> —LUKE 21:11, NKJV

As the final judgment of God begins to be fulfilled upon this globe, earthquakes will play a more important and increasing role in what is called the end times.

Earthquakes, also called tremors, are not just physical phenomena. Sometimes God has caused earthquakes to pronounce His presence:

> Tremble, O earth, at the presence of the Lord, at the presence of the God of Jacob...
>
> —PSALM 114:7, NIV

> The mountains quake before him and the hills melt away. The earth trembles at his presence, the world and all who live in it.
>
> —NAHUM 1:5, NIV

It has been told in the Holy Scriptures that God will also use earthquakes to signify God's wrath upon the world for rejecting His admonitions and correction.

> But the LORD is the true God, he is the living God, and an everlasting king: at his wrath the earth shall tremble, and the nations shall not be able to abide his indignation.
>
> —JEREMIAH 10:10, KJV

> Then the earth shook and trembled; the foundations also of the hills moved and were shaken, because he was wroth.
>
> —Psalm 18:7, kjv

Earthquakes are mentioned a lot in the Book of Revelation. In fact, the Book of Revelation prophesies of five specific earthquakes:

1. Earthquakes are first mentioned in Revelation in chapter 6:

> And I beheld when he had opened the sixth seal, and, lo, there was a great earthquake; and the sun became black as sackcloth of hair, and the moon became as blood…
>
> —Revelation 6:12, kjv

> And every mountain and island were moved out of their places.
>
> —Revelation 6:14b, kjv

2. In Revelation 8, we read:

> And the angel took the censer, and filled it with fire of the altar, and cast it into the earth: and there were voices, and thunderings, and lightnings, and an earthquake.
>
> —Revelation 8:5, kjv

3. Another earthquake precedes and announces the climactic return of Christ.

> And they heard a great voice from heaven saying unto them [the two witnesses], Come up hither. And they

> ascended up to heaven in a cloud; and their enemies beheld them.
>
> And the same hour was there a great earthquake, and the tenth part of the city fell, and in the earthquake were slain of men seven thousand: and the remnant were affrighted, and gave glory to the God of heaven.
>
> —REVELATION 11:12–13, KJV

4. This next earthquake happens right after the return of Christ.

> And the temple of God was opened in heaven, and there was seen in his temple the ark of his testament: and there were lightnings, and voices, and thunderings, and an earthquake, and great hail.
>
> —REVELATION 11:19, KJV

5. The final earthquake prophesied in Revelation will be the most powerful one to ever be experienced upon the face of the earth.

> And the seventh angel poured out his vial into the air; and there came a great voice out of the temple of heaven, from the throne, saying, It is done.
>
> And there were voices, and thunders, and lightnings; and there was a great earthquake, such as was not since men were upon the earth, so mighty an earthquake, and so great.
>
> —REVELATION 16:17–18, KJV

This powerful earthquake will literally change the topography of the earth, as told in the Bible:

> And every island fled away, and the mountains were not found.
>
> —Revelation 16:20, kjv

One of the voices that trumpet the prophetic word of earthquakes at the end-time is the Pastor General of the Restored Church of God, Pastor David C. Pack. He is the Editor-in-Chief of the monthly magazine, *The Real Truth,* and also hosts the television program *The World to Come.* Pastor Pack founded the Restored Church of God in 1999 when they separated from the Worldwide Church of God.

In March 2010, Pastor General Pack wrote an article entitled, "Earthquakes and Volcanoes—Their Role in Prophecy," from which this is an excerpt:

> The God of all power, who formed the hills and mountains, will reform them and reshape the surface of this planet (Amos 4:13; Ps. 90:2).
>
> Notice Isaiah 40:4–5: "Every valley shall be exalted, and every mountain and hill shall be made low: and the crooked shall be made straight, and the rough places plain: and the glory of the Lord shall be revealed, and all flesh shall see it together: for the mouth of the Lord has spoken it."
>
> These verses speak of dramatic changes in the earth's surface. Vast mountain ranges will no longer exist. Any remaining mountains and hills will be used for a special purpose as God has appointed.
>
> The renewal of the surface of the earth will be to accommodate the vast number of humanity that will populate the earth by the later stages of the Millennium and also the many billions that will

come up later in the general resurrection—the White Throne Judgment (Rev. 20:11).

The earth will be able to accommodate many more billions at that time once more usable land becomes available for farming and for living space.

Not only will mountain ranges be removed, more land will be reclaimed from the deserts and oceans as well. These changes in the topography of the earth will accommodate a change in the weather. It will become favorable, rather than the harsh, threatening destructive element as has been the case throughout human history.

Without droughts and floods, and without the terrible extremes of temperature, precipitation, and destruction from other elements in nature, farming will be more productive. Even the waters of the oceans will be healed and purified (Ezek. 47:8–10).

Earthquakes have been instrumental in serving God's purpose in a number of ways. Indeed there is a purpose for every aspect of God's creation: "To everything there is a season, and a time to every purpose under the heaven" (Eccles. 3:1).

The good news beyond the depressing trends and statistics of this present world will eventually eclipse the human tragedies that occur in this age. Earthquakes will play a role in this transition that ends in peace, security, and fulfillment for the entire world.

As frightening and destructive as they are, God will use earthquakes to reshape the earth's surface, in preparation for the greatest time of peace and abundance that mankind has ever known.

This is a time that the whole world can look forward to. And it is coming soon![3]

Endnotes

1. See http://en.wikipedia.org/wiki/Earthquake.
2. See http://earthquake.usgs.gov/learn/facts.php.
3. See http://realtruth.org/articles/090907-006-weather.html.

Chapter 1

CURRENT PHENOMENA AND QUAKE FAULT LINES

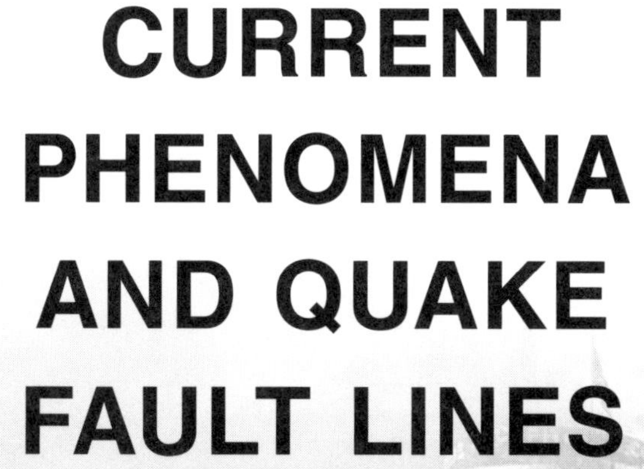

We remember watching the third game of the 1989 World Series. It was between the San Francisco Giants and the Oakland Raiders. On October 17, we were glued to our television sets, just like millions of others. Just minutes before the opening pitch, a 6.9 magnitude earthquake struck the Bay Area causing major damage and some deaths within San Francisco and Oakland.

We watched in disbelief as we saw the ground shake and the cameras wobble, with players and fans running for cover. It seemed so surreal. Candlestick Park suffered damage. The power was knocked out. Out of very real concerns for the public safety of the people in the ballpark, the game was postponed. The series resumed 11 days later.

How could we forget the two levels of a major Interstate highway being flattened like a pancake, trapping several cars and people? It was the first time most people had ever experienced an earthquake in real time. Millions were affected by this live broadcast nationwide of a major earthquake. Earthquakes seem to be just a way of life to those living in California.

On March 29, 2014, *The Washington Post* reported on a Magnitude-5.1 earthquake shaking Los Angeles:

> A moderate earthquake that rattled a swath of Southern California forced several dozen people in one community out of their homes and apartments

after firefighters discovered foundation problems that made the buildings unsafe to enter, authorities said Saturday.

Fire inspectors red-tagged 20 apartment units in a building in the Orange County city of Fullerton after finding a major foundation crack. Structural woes included broken and leaning chimneys were uncovered in half a dozen single-family homes, which were also deemed as unsafe to occupy until building inspectors clear the structures. The damage displaced 83 residents.

Despite the evacuations, Friday night's magnitude-5.1 quake centered about 25 miles south of downtown Los Angeles mostly just frayed nerves....

Residents were inconvenienced and some lost valuables, but "thankfully the damage wasn't greater," said Chi-Chung Keung, a spokesman for the city of Fullerton.

Business owners in Orange County spent the aftermath sweeping up shattered glass and restocking shelves. Utility crews worked to restore power and shut off gas leaks and repair water main breaks. A rock slide led to the closure of a road in the Carbon Canyon area of nearby Brea.

Friday's jolt was the strongest to strike the greater Los Angeles region since 2008. Southern California has been in a seismic lull since the deadly 1994 Northridge earthquake killed several dozen people and caused $25 billion in damage.

The latest quake hit a week after a magnitude-4.4 centered in the San Fernando Valley shook buildings and rattled nerves....

U.S. Geological Survey seismologist Lucy Jones said it's unclear whether Southern California is entering a

> more active seismic period. "We have been in a really quiet time. It can't stay that way," Jones said.[1]

News reports like this in Southern California are standard fare as the number and intensity of California earthquakes increase. As you will read throughout this book, earthquakes are a decisive sign of the end times.

Earthquakes are worldwide in scope. For instance, on April 1, 2014, a magnitude-8.2 earthquake struck northern Chile. *The New York Times* published an article entitled "Earthquake Hits off Coast of Northern Chile" regarding the event:

> An 8.2-magnitude earthquake struck off the coast of northern Chile on Tuesday night, forcing a massive evacuation along the country's long coastline. At least five people were reported to have died.
>
> The first waves of a tsunami hit several cities along the coast, which extends 2,653 miles.
>
> The epicenter of the earthquake was in waters 53 miles southwest of Cuya, a small town in Arica Province near the border with Peru. The deaths—four men and one woman, all in the city of Iquique—were the result of heart attacks or crushing, Interior Minister Rodrigo Peñailillo said. At least three people in Iquique, which has a population of about 182,000, were also reported injured.
>
> The national emergency service ordered the immediate evacuation of all coastal areas throughout the country, including Easter Island and the archipelago of Juan Fernández.
>
> More waves were expected throughout the night, with the highest expected to reach eight feet, near Iquique, Chilean officials said. According to a Reuters

> report, the Pacific Tsunami Warning Center said the coasts of Peru, Ecuador, Colombia, Panama, Costa Rica and Nicaragua were also at risk....
>
> Chile lies in one of the world's most earthquake-prone zones. An 8.8-magnitude earthquake in 2010 off the coast of central Chile left at least 525 people dead. In 1960, a 9.5-magnitude earthquake, thought to be the largest of the 20th century, hit near Chile's coast near the city of Valdivia; the disaster left about 1,600 people dead, largely from a tsunami caused by the earthquake.
>
> About 300 earthquakes of varying magnitude have shaken Chile's northern coast in several weeks, delivering an unusual surge in seismic activity in the region. Since the 2010 earthquake, Chilean authorities have sought to improve evacuation procedures.[2]

Before we dive into the Scriptures and various prophecies and learn from several godly prophets, we wanted to give you the news media side, which you've just read.

FAULT LINES

We are going to make this particular portion short and to the point. We do not pretend to be seismic experts. But experts say that those most vulnerable to earthquakes live on fault lines. For instance, Californians are accustomed to the term "San Andreas fault line," which runs through California and makes that state the most vulnerable to the greatest number of earthquakes.

> The San Andreas Fault is a continental transform fault that extends roughly (1,300 km) 810 miles through California. It forms the tectonic boundary

> between the Pacific Plate and the North American Plate, and its motion is right-lateral strike-slip (horizontal). The fault divides into three segments, each with different characteristics and a different degree of earthquake risk.
>
> The fault was first identified in 1895 by Professor Andrew Lawson from UC Berkeley who discovered the northern zone. It is named after the Sand Andreas Lake, a small body of water that was formed in a valley between the two plates. Following the 1906 San Francisco Earthquake, Lawson concluded that the fault extended all the way into southern California. In 1953, geologist Thomas Dibblee astounded the scientific establishment with his conclusion that hundreds of miles of lateral movement could occur along the fault.[3]

California's vulnerability to quakes has also given rise to several prophets saying that parts of the state will eventually "slip into the Pacific Ocean." Those comments revolve around the fault lines that run through California. For instance, on January 8, 2014, *The Los Angeles Times* reported,

> New state geological maps released Wednesday show that several major Hollywood developments are much closer to an active earthquake fault than city officials have said.[4]

This vulnerable area includes the Hollywood landmark of the headquarters of Capitol Records.

However, as recently as May 7, 2015, in an article entitled, "U.S. Quake Damage Is a Risk that Goes Way beyond Californians," the *Los Angeles Times* observed,

> People living in California and the West Coast still face the highest earthquake risk. But a new study says we are not alone.
>
> That report found that close to half of all Americans—nearly 150 million people—are threatened by shaking from earthquakes strong enough to cause damage.
>
> That figure is a sharp jump from the figure in 1994, when the Federal Emergency Management Agency estimated that just 75 million Americans were at risk from earthquakes.
>
> One reason for the sharp increase in exposure to quake damage is population increases in areas prone to earthquakes, especially California, said William Leith, a co-author and USGS senior science advisor for earthquake and geologic hazards....
>
> Authorities calculated that the average financial loss to earthquakes in the lower 48 states is roughly $4.5 billion a year, mainly in California, Oregon and Washington.....
>
> The numbers did not factor in the greater number of earthquakes that scientists say are occurring because of human activity.
>
> Those earthquakes have increased in some parts of the eastern and central United States as wastewater is injected deep underground. Oklahoma has suffered the greatest number of man-made earthquakes in recent years, scientists say....
>
> In California, the greatest risk for a big earthquake is considered to be the San Andreas Fault, which is the state's largest and fastest-moving fault.[5]

Obviously, the current quake fault lines are ominous to those who live there. The vulnerability of these areas puts many completely at risk. God's people have prophesied, as you will read, but our great God is one of victory!

ENDNOTES

1. See http://www.washingtonpost.com/national/health-science/magnitude-51-earthquake-shakes-los-angeles-displaces-some-residents/2014/03/29/dff2a69c-b770-11e3-8cc3-d4bf596577eb_story.html.
2. See http://www.nytimes.com/2014/04/02/world/americas/earthquake-hits-off-coast-of-north-chile.html?_r=0.
3. See https://en.wikipedia.org/wiki/San_Andreas_Fault.
4. See http://www.latimes.com/local/lanow/la-me-ln-hollywood-developments-straddle-quake-fault-maps-20140108-story.html.
5. See http://www.latimes.com/local/california/la-me-faults-20150507-story.html.

Chapter 2

ST. HILDEGARD: PROPHECIES ABOUT THE USA

ONE OF THE very earliest prophecies regarding earthquakes goes back nearly nine centuries. It comes from Saint Hildegard of the Catholic Church. St. Hildegard was a devout teacher. This was during a time in the Catholic Church when women were not really considered teachers.

Many have discounted Hildegard and her teachings because holistic practitioners and those in the New Age movement follow her. However, she is revered by many Catholics. Even Pope Benedict XVI has stood up for her. In 2012, Pope Benedict XVI officially declared Hildegard a saint:

> Hildegard of Bingen was from Germany. She's mostly known for her religious visions and prophecies. She lived in the XI and XII century, but even so, her message is still quite alive. The Pope has talked about her and her message in two general audiences.
>
> Also, in coming months, the Pope is considering declaring her a Doctor of the Church for her high intelligence and feminine sensibility.
>
> St. Hildegard was one of the most active women of her time. She wrote about theology and morals, but also about medicine and science. She even found the time to compose 78 musical pieces.[1]

Saint Hildegard was a prolific writer, and her works (which include 9 books and over one hundred letters, as well as 70 poems and 72 songs) have been studied extensively by modern historians.

One of the oldest prophecies concerning the United States goes back almost 840 years ago and was given by Saint Hildegard.

Irene B. Hahn at Unity Publishing writes,

> At a time when few women wrote, Hildegard produced major works of theology and visionary writings. When few women were accorded respect, she was consulted by and advised bishops, popes, and kings.... Although not yet canonized, Hildegard has been beatified, and is frequently referred to as Saint Hildegard....
>
> In 1141, a vision of God gave Hildegard instant understanding of the meaning of the religious texts....
>
> "Before the Comet comes, many nations, the good excepted, will be scoured with want and famine. The great nation [many have interpreted this to mean the United States of America] in the ocean that is inhabited by people of different tribes and descent by an earthquake, storm and tidal waves will be devastated. It will be divided, and in great part submerged. That nation will also have many misfortunes at sea, and lose its colonies in the east through a Tiger and a Lion.
>
> The Comet by its tremendous pressure will force much out of the ocean and flood many countries, causing much want and many plagues. [After the] great Comet, the great nation will be devastated by earthquakes, storms, and great waves of water, causing much want and plagues. The ocean will also flood many other countries, so that all coastal cities will live in fear, with many destroyed. All sea

> coast cities will be fearful and many of them will be destroyed by tidal waves, and most living creatures will be killed and even those who escape will die from a horrible disease. For in none of these cities does a person live according to the laws of God.
>
> [Her many] writings were submitted to the bishop (Henry, 1145–53) and clergy of Mainz, who pronounced them as coming from God.... Albero of Chiny, Bishop of Verdun, was commissioned to investigate and made a favorable report.[2]

Before this time, there were hardly any recorded prophecies involving earthquakes, the end times, and cataclysmic events. St. Hildegard was a true pioneer, especially in the Catholic Church. St. Hildegard has reserved for herself the title of "Saint" because of her acute diligence to perceive the future, which includes earthquakes.

Endnotes

1. See http://www.romereports.com/2012/05/10/benedict-xvi-officially-declares-hildegard-of-bingen-a-saint.
2. See http://www.unitypublishing.com/prophecy/Hildigard Saint.htm.

Chapter 3

EARTHQUAKE PROPHECIES BY MOTHER SHIPTON

TO SOME, URSULA Southeil, or Mother Shipton, was legendary. To others, she was just a myth. But her prophecies sincerely rattled people in England during the mid-1500s.

As a prophetess, she was looked at by many as being the "16th century's female Nostradamus" of England. Her outrageous (at the time) prophecies were revered and trusted for many years. Spotty historical records and references put her life between 1488 and 1561.

According to a website maintained by Susan Larison Danz, who is the host of *The Frontier beyond Fear* online radio program,

> The name Shipton shows up earlier than any reference to Soothtell, with its first known historical reference from 1641 in a pamphlet by Lownds, still many years after her death, where she is referred to as "Shipton's wife." A very popular (though not always accurate) account of Mother Shipton's life first published in 1667 by Irish writer Richard Head assigns the name "Shipton" to Agatha Shipton, in this account said to be the mother of Mother Shipton. And one cannot discount the oral tradition surrounding Mother Shipton, begun by many who were illiterate around the time of her lifetime and kept alive until the present day.[1]

Let us introduce you to some of the major prophecies, written in verse, by Mother Shipton in Yorkshire, England, from the mid sixteenth century:

> Yet greater sign there be to see; as man nears latter century. Three sleeping mountains gather breath, and spew out mud, ice and death. An earthquake swallow town and town; in lands as yet to me unknown. And Christian one fights Christian two and nations sigh, yet nothing do. And yellow men great power gain; from a mighty bear with whom they've lain.
>
> [Volcanoes, earthquakes (in unknown land—America?) destroying town after town, fighting between nations. Speaks of a Chinese (yellow)—Russian (bear) alliance against the west. Most of China's current weapons have come in deals with Russia.]....
>
> For storms will rage and oceans roar when Gabriel stands on sea and shore, and as he blows his wondrous horn, old worlds die and new be born....
>
> For seven days and seven nights, man will watch this awesome sight. The tides will rise beyond their ken. To bite away the shores and then the mountains will begin to roar and earthquakes split the plain to shore.
>
> [After asteroid hits in the oceans, huge tidal waves will strike followed by awakening of volcanoes and earthquakes.]....
>
> And lands will crack and rend anew. Do you think it strange? It will come true![2]

Mother Shipton was literally a prophetess "before her time." Her keen insights, from the mid-1500s, are well attuned to the current times. It is advisable to take her prophecies seriously.

Endnotes

1. See www.mothershipton.com/history.html.
2. See http://www.bibliotecapleyades.net/esp_shipton01.htm.

Chapter 4

JOE BRANDT'S DREAM OF THE CALIFORNIA EARTHQUAKE

WHO, EXACTLY, IS Joe Brandt?

Joseph W. Brandt served in the United States Army, enlisting in 1944. He lived quite a fulfilling life (November 19, 1919—July 5, 1995). In 1937, at the age of 17, he experienced extreme head injuries when he fell from his horse. At that time, he began to receive a series of prophetic dreams about a mega-earthquake to hit California in the future, sinking Los Angeles, and much of California and Japan.

In a powerful article entitled, "The Coming Earthquake," Jessica Madigan (Mei Ling) gives an account of Joe Brandt and his astonishing dreams:

> On Christmas Eve, in 1965, my husband—my closest friend, Fran Brandt, and her husband, Joe, were celebrating with sandwiches, coffee, and fruit cake, in the meditation room, downstairs. Carols poured from the TV, upstairs, a holiday dinner was in the making. For some reason, Joe Fran's husband—ventured to speak of the coming California earthquake. It did not seem a moment to talk about earthquakes—because Christmas is the most precious time in the world. The huge tree, ablaze with tiny star-lights seemed to presage only goodness, and love, and beauty. Joe was saying that he had an accident—a fall from a horse when he was 17, and for days he had a concussion. During this period, a continuous dream came again and again—as if he were viewing a tremendous

earthquake and inundation in California and other parts of the world.

I listened—politely—made some comment, and turned to talk to Fran about a new movie—or some equally world shaking event. I was vaguely aware that Joe had brought in a sheaf of papers—and he said he would put it in my downstairs desk [in 1965] until I had time to read the "dream." That time did not arrive, until, by accident, I came across them this last week [in 1967]—pages after pages after pages—written in a boy's handwriting, about the coming California earthquake. It would take weeks to research all this material—but I phoned my former geology professor and read portions to him. *Could this happen? Could California go down in just this way? Would other areas be affected in a matter of hours?* He answered in the affirmative. Joe had written (sleeping and dreaming—and in drowsy awakening) about positions of various *faults,* strata of rock, earth movements, so much material that a geologist of many years would scarcely attempt such a work [this geological data was omitted from Jessica's book]. Yet—here it was—waiting for me to find it for two years. Since that night, Fran has changed worlds [in 1966 or 1967]—and my husband is very ill—other unforeseen events which I could not have imagined have taken place—and all this, perhaps, precluded my finding of the "earthquake papers."

This book is already very long—double its size—and I realize that this vision given to a 17 year old boy must be placed, as it is, into a book. Consciously, he knew nothing of geology or of the possibility of a coming earthquake. The notes are 30 years old—yellowed with age—and yet there is a clarity and an unbelievable reality in them. Some of the highlights must be given—because, I am certain now, as I was not certain on Christmas Eve of 1965, that the California earthquake WILL come...and its coming is close at hand. Since Joe covered the *areas around the world which would be affected,* not all of these can be given (although perhaps we can write a booklet on this experience), but for those of us in *this land*...especially the *California land,* these are the highlights of that vision.

I woke up in the hospital room with a terrific headache—as if the whole world was revolving inside my brain. I remember, vaguely, the fall from my horse—Blackie. As I lay there, pictures began to form in my mind—pictures that stood still. I seemed to be in another world. Whether it was the future, or it was some ancient land, I could not say. Then slowly, like the silver screen of the "talkies," but with color and smell and sound, I seemed to find myself in Los Angeles—but I swear it was much bigger, and buses and odd-shaped cars crowded the city streets.

I thought about Hollywood Boulevard, and I found myself there. Whether this is true, I do not know, but there were a lot of guys my age with beards and wearing, some of them, earrings. All the girls, some of them keen-o, wore real short skirts...and they slouched along—moving like a dance. Yet they seemed familiar. I wondered if I could talk to them, and I said, "Hello," but they didn't see or hear me. I decided I would look as funny to them as they looked to me. I guess it is something you have to learn. I couldn't do it.

I noticed there was a quietness about the air, a kind of stillness. Something else was missing, something that should be there. At first, I couldn't figure it out, I didn't know what it was—then I did. There were no birds. I listened. I walked two blocks north of the Boulevard—all houses—no birds. I wondered what had happened to them. Had they gone away? Again, I could hear the stillness. Then I knew something was going to happen.

I wondered what year it was. It certainly was not 1937. I saw a newspaper on the corner with a picture of the President. It surely wasn't Mr. Roosevelt. He was bigger, heavier, big ears.

If it wasn't 1937, I wondered what year it was... My eyes weren't working right. Someone was coming—someone in 1937—it was that darned, fat nurse ready to take my temperature. I woke up. Crazy dream.

The next day: Gosh, my headache is worse. It is a wonder I didn't get killed on that horse. I've had another crazy dream, back in Hollywood. Those people. Why do they dress like that, I wonder? Funny glow about them. It is a shine around their heads—something shining. I remember it now. I found myself back on the Boulevard. I was waiting for something to happen and I was going to be there. I looked up at the clock down by that big theater. It was ten minutes to four. Something big was going to happen.

I wondered if I went into a movie (since nobody could see me) if I'd like it. Some cardboard blond was draped over the marquee with her leg six feet long. I started to go in, but it wasn't inside. I was waiting for something to happen outside. I walked down the street. In the concrete they have names of stars. I just recognized a few of them. The other names I had never heard. I was getting bored, I wanted to get back to the hospital in Fresno, and I wanted to stay there on the Boulevard, even if nobody could see me. Those crazy kids. Why are they dressed like that? Maybe it is some big Halloween doings, but it don't [sic] seem like Halloween. More like early spring. There was that sound again, that lack of sound. Stillness, stillness, stillness. The quiet is getting bigger and bigger. I know it is going to happen. Something is going to happen. It is happening now! It sure did. She woke me up, grinning and smiling, that fat one again.

"It's time for your milk, kiddo," she says. Gosh, old women of thirty acting like the cat's pajamas. Next time maybe she'll bring hot chocolate.

Where have I been? Where haven't I been? I've been to the ends of the earth and back. I've been to the end of the world—there isn't anything left. Not even Fresno, even though I'm lying here right this minute. If only my eyes would get a little clearer so I can write all this down. Nobody will believe me, anyway. I'm going back to that last moment on the Boulevard. Some sweet kid went past, dragging little boys (twins, I guess) by each hand. Her skirt was up—well, pretty high—and she had a tired look. I thought for a minute I could ask her about the birds, what had happened to them, and then I remembered she hadn't seen me. Her hair was all frowzy, way out all over her head. A lot of them looked like that, but she looked so tired and like she was sorry about something. I guess she was sorry before it happened—because it surely did happen. There was a funny smell. I don't know where it came from. I didn't like it. A smell like sulfur, sulfuric acid, a smell like death. For a minute I thought I was back in chem. [Chemistry class].

When I looked around for the girl, she was gone. I wanted to find her for some reason. It was as if I knew something was going to happen and I could stay with her, help her. She was gone, and I walked half a block, then I saw the clock again. My eyes seemed glued to that clock. I couldn't move. I just waited. It was five minutes to four on a sunny afternoon. I thought I would stand there looking at that clock forever waiting for something to come. Then, when it came, it was nothing. It was just nothing. It wasn't nearly as hard as the earthquake we had two years ago. The ground shook, just an instant. People looked at each other, surprised. Then they laughed. I laughed, too. So this was what I had been waiting for. This funny little shake. It meant nothing.

I was relieved and I was disappointed. What had I been waiting for? I started back up the Boulevard, moving my legs like those kids. How do they do it? I never found out. I felt as if the ground wasn't solid under me, knew I was dreaming, and yet I wasn't dreaming. There was that smell again, coming up from the ocean. I was getting to the 5 and 10 store and I saw the look on the kids' faces. Two of them were right in front of me, coming my way.

"Let's get out of this place. Let's go back East." He seemed scared. It wasn't as if the sidewalks were trembling—but you couldn't seem to see them. Not with your eyes you couldn't. An old lady had a dog, a little white dog, and she stopped and looked scared, and grabbed him in her arms and said: "Let's go home, Frou Frou. Mama is going to take you home." That poor lady, hanging on to her dog.

I got scared. Real scared. I remembered the girl. She was way down the block, probably. I ran and ran, and the ground kept trembling. I couldn't see it. I couldn't see it. But I knew it was trembling. Everybody looked scared. They looked terrible. One young lady just sat down on the sidewalk all doubled up. She kept saying, *"earthquake; it's the earthquake,"* over and over. But I couldn't see that anything was different.

Then, when it came, how it came. Like nothing in God's world. Like nothing. It was like the scream of a siren, long and low, or the scream of a woman I heard having a baby when I was a kid. It was awful. It was as if something—some monster—was pushing up the sidewalks. You felt it long before you saw it, as if the sidewalks wouldn't hold you anymore. I looked out at the cars. They were honking, but not scared. They just kept moving. They didn't seem to know yet that anything was happening. Then, that white car, that baby half-sized one came sprawling from the inside lane right against the curb. The girl who was driving just sat there. She sat there with her eyes staring, as if she couldn't move, but I could hear her. She made funny noises.

I watched her, thinking of the other girl. I said that it was a dream and I would wake up. But I didn't wake up. The shaking had started again, but this time different. It was a nice shaking, like a cradle being rocked for a minute, and then I saw the middle of the Boulevard seem to be breaking in two. The concrete looked as if it were being pushed straight up by some giant shovel. It was breaking in two. That is why the girl's car went out of control. And then a loud sound again, like I've never heard before—then hundreds of sounds—all kinds of sounds; children, and women, and those crazy guys with earrings. They were all moving, some of them above the sidewalk. I can't describe it. They were lifted up.

The waters kept oozing—oozing. The cries. God, it was awful. I woke up. I never want to have that dream again.

It came again. Like the first time which was a preview and all I could remember was that it was the end of the world. I was right back there—all that crying. Right in the middle of it. My eardrums felt as if they were going to burst. Noise everywhere. People falling down, some of them hurt badly. Pieces of buildings, chips, flying in the air. One hit me hard on the side of the face, but I didn't seem to feel it. I wanted to wake up, to get away from this place. It had been fun in the beginning, the first dream, when I kind of knew I was going to dream the end of the world or something. This was terrible. There were older people in cars. Most of the kids were on the street. But those old guys were yelling bloody murder, as if anybody could help them. Nobody could help anybody. It was then I felt myself lifted up. Maybe I had died. I don't know. But I was over the city. It was tilting toward the ocean—like a picnic table.

The buildings were holding, better than you could believe. They were holding. They were holding. They were holding.

The people saw they were holding and they tried to cling to them or get inside. It was fantastic. Like a building had a will of its own. Everything else breaking around them, and they were holding, holding. I was up over them—looking down. I started to root for them. "Hold that line," I said. "Hold that line. Hold that line. Hold that line." I wanted to cheer, to shout, to scream. If the buildings held, those buildings on the Boulevard, maybe the girl—the girl with the two kids—maybe she could get inside. It looked that way for a long time, maybe three minutes, and three minutes was like forever. You knew they were going to hold, even if the waters kept coming up. Only they didn't.

I've never imagined what it would be like for a building to die. A building dies just like a person. It gives way, some of the bigger ones did just that. They began to crumble, like an old man with palsy, who couldn't take it anymore. They crumbled right down to nothing. And the little ones screamed like mad—over and above the roar of the people. They were mad about dying. But buildings die.

I couldn't look anymore at the people. I kept wanting to get higher. Then I seemed to be out of it all, but I could see. I seemed to be up on Big Bear near San Bernardino, but the funny thing was that I could see everywhere. I knew what was happening. The earth seemed to start to tremble again. I could feel it even though I was high up. This time it lasted maybe twelve seconds, and it was gentle. You couldn't believe anything so gentle could cause so much damage. But then I saw the streets of Los Angeles—and everything between the San Bernardino Mountains and Los Angeles. It was still tilting towards the ocean, houses, everything that was left. I could see the big lanes—dozens of big lanes still loaded with cars sliding the same way. Now the ocean was coming in, moving like a huge snake across the land. I wondered how long it was, and I could see the clock, even though I wasn't there on the Boulevard. It was 4:29. It had been half an hour. I was glad I couldn't hear the crying anymore. But I could see everything. I could see everything.

Then, like looking at a huge map of the world, I could see what was happening on the land and with the people. San Francisco was feeling it, but she was not in any way like Hollywood or Los Angeles. It was moving just like that earthquake movie with Jeanette McDonald and Gable. I could see all those mountains coming together...I knew it was going to happen to San Francisco—it was going to turn over—it would turn upside down. It went quickly, because of the twisting, I guess. It seemed much faster than Hollywood, but then I wasn't exactly there. I was a long way off. I was a long, long way off. I shut my eyes for a long time—I guess ten minutes—and when I opened them I saw Grand Canyon.

When I looked at Grand Canyon, that great big gap was closing in, and Boulder Dam was being pushed, from underneath. And then, Nevada, and on up to Reno. Way down south, way down. Baja, California. Mexico, too. It looked like some volcano down there was erupting, along with everything else. I saw the map of South America, especially Colombia. Another volcano—eruption—shaking violently. I seemed to be seeing a movie of three months before—before the Hollywood earthquake. Venezuela seemed to be having some kind of volcanic activity. Away off in the distance, I could see Japan, on a fault, too. It was so far off—not easy to see because I was still on Big Bear Mountain, but it started to go into the sea. I couldn't hear screaming, but I could see the surprised look on their faces. They looked so surprised. Japanese girls are made well, supple, easy, muscles that move well. Pretty, too. But they were all like dolls. It was so far away I could hardly see it. In a minute or two it seemed over. Everybody was gone. There was nobody left.

[Brother Branham said: "Japan...she's ready to rock to pieces right now. And there's no way you can stop it, because they have neglected to do exactly what God told them to do. Instead of preach of Gospel, they have built buildings, and had fine scholarships, and educations."]

I didn't know time now. I couldn't see a clock. I tried to see the island of Hawaii. I could see huge tidal waves beating against it. The people on the streets were getting wet, and they were scared. But I didn't see anybody go into the sea.

I seemed way around the globe. More flooding. Is the world going to be drenched? Constantinople. Black Sea rising. Suez Canal, for some reason seemed to be drying up. Sicily—she doesn't hold. I could see a map. Mt. Etna. Mt. Etna is shaking. A lot of area seemed to go, but it seemed to be earlier or later. I wasn't sure of time, now.

England—huge floods—but no tidal waves. Water, water everywhere, but no one was going into the sea. People were frightened and crying. Some places they fell to the streets on their knees and started to pray for the world. I didn't know the English were emotional. Ireland, Scotland—all kinds of churches were crowded—it seemed night and day. People were carrying candles and everybody was crying for California, Nevada, parts of Colorado—maybe even all of it, even Utah. Everybody was crying—most of them didn't even know anybody in California, Nevada, Utah, but they were crying as if they were blood kin. Like one family. Like it happened to them.

New York was coming into view—she was still there, nothing had happened, yet water level was way up. Here, things were different. People were running in the streets yelling—"end of the world." Kids ran into restaurants and ate everything in sight. I saw a shoe store with all the shoes gone in about five minutes. 5th Avenue—everybody running. Some radio blasting—bigger—a loud speaker—that in a few minutes, power might be shut off. They must control themselves. Five girls were running like mad toward the YMCA, that place on Lexington or somewhere. But nothing was happening in New York. I saw an old lady with garbage cans filling them with water. Everybody seemed scared to death. Some people looked dazed. The streets seemed filled with loud speakers. It wasn't daylight. It was night.

I saw, like the next day, and everything was topsy-turvy. Loud speakers again about fuel tanks broken in areas—shortage of oil. People seemed to be looting markets.

I saw a lot of places that seemed safe, and people were not so scared. Especially the rural areas. Here everything was almost as if nothing had happened. People seemed headed to these places, some on foot, some in cars that still had fuel. I heard—or somehow I knew—that somewhere in the Atlantic land had come up. A lot of land. I was getting awfully tired. I wanted to wake up. I wanted to go back to the girl—to know where she was—and those two kids. I found myself back in Hollywood—and it was still 4:29. I wasn't up on Big Bear at all, I was perched over Hollywood. I was just there. It seemed perfectly natural in my dream.

I could hear now. I could hear, someplace, a radio station blasting out—telling people not to panic. They were dying in the streets. There were picture stations with movies—some right in Hollywood—these were carrying on with all the shaking. One fellow in the picture station was a little short guy who should have been scared to death. But he wasn't. He kept shouting and reading instructions. Something about helicopters or planes would go over—some kind of planes—but I knew they couldn't. Things were happening in the atmosphere. The waves were rushing up now. Waves. Such waves. Nightmare waves.

Then, I saw again. Boulder Dam, going down—pushing together, pushing together breaking apart—no, Grand Canyon was pushing together, and Boulder Dam was breaking apart. It was still daylight. All these radio stations went off at the same time—Boulder Dam had broken.

I wondered how everybody would know about it—people back East. That was when I saw the "ham radio operators." I saw them in the strangest places, as if I were right there with them. Like the little guy with glasses, they kept sounding the alarm. One kept saying: "This is California. We are going into the sea. This is California. We are going into the sea. Get to high places. Get to the mountains. All states west—this is California. We are going into the...we are going into the..." I thought he was going to say "sea," but I could see him. He was inland, but the waters had come in. His hand was still clinging to the table. He was trying to get up, so that once again he could say: "This is California. We are going into the sea. This is California. We are going into the sea."

I seemed to hear this, over and over, for what seemed hours—just those words—they kept it up until the last minute—all of them calling out, "Get to the mountains—this is California. We are going into the sea."

I woke up. It didn't seem as if I had been dreaming. I have never been so tired. For a minute or two, I thought it had happened. I wondered about two things. I hadn't seen what happened to Fresno and I hadn't found out what happened to that girl.

I've been thinking about it all morning. I'm going home tomorrow. It was just a dream. It was nothing more. Nobody in the future on Hollywood Boulevard is going to be wearing earrings—and those beards. Nothing like that is ever going to happen. That girl was so real to me—that girl with those kids. It won't ever happen—but if it did, how could I tell her (maybe she isn't even born yet) to move away from California when she has her twins—and she can't be on the Boulevard that day. She was so gosh-darned real.

The other thing—those ham operators—hanging on like that—over and over—saying the same thing:

"This is California. We are going into the sea. This is California. We are going into the sea. Get to the mountains. Get to the hilltops. California, Nevada, Colorado, Arizona, Utah. This is California. We are going into the sea."

I guess I'll hear that for days.[1]

The following is a different perspective on Joe Brandt's dreams. William Branham wrote the following in his book, *Trying to Do God a Service without Being in the Will of God:*

> A prophecy that I made about 1935 or something like that, said: "The time would come…that the sea would weep its way into the desert." Look what'll take place. If that thousands of square miles falls down into the lava of the earth and slides in, there'll be millions die at one time. And that'll cause such

a tidal wave... Remember, plumb up into the Salton Sea is a hundred or two hundred feet lower than the sea level. That water will probably come almost to Tucson with that tidal wave coming across there. And the sea shall weep its way into the desert.

[The Spirit of the Lord came upon the Prophet as he was preaching in Los Angeles]: "We don't know what time. And you don't know what time that this city one day is going to be laying out here in the bottom of this ocean."

"O, Capernaum," said Jesus, "Thou who exalted into heaven will be brought down into hell, for if the mighty works had been done in Sodom and Gomorrah, it'd have been standing till this day." And Sodom and Gomorrah lays at the bottom of the Dead Sea, and Capernaum's in the bottom of the sea. Thou city, who claims to be the city of the Angels, who's exalted yourself into heaven and sent all the dirty filthy things of fashions and things, till even the foreign countries come here to pick up our filth and send it away, with your fine churches and steeples, and so forth the way you do; remember, one day you'll be laying in the bottom of this sea. You're great honeycomb under you right now. The wrath of God is belching right beneath you. How much longer He'll hold this sandbar hanging over that, when that ocean out yonder a mile deep will slide in there plumb back to the Salton Sea. It'll be worse than the last day of Pompeii. Repent, Los Angeles. Repent the rest of you and turn to God. The hour of His wrath is upon the earth. Flee while there's time to flee and come into Christ. "Let us pray" ("Choosing a Bride," 3–5).

> [And again]: The last meeting I had in California, while speaking, and didn't know nothing happened till I got on the street, It told California, said, "Capernaum, Capernaum, the city that's called by the name of the angels (that's Los Angeles), you've exalted yourself into heaven, but you'll be brought down into hell. For if the mighty works had been done in Sodom that's been done in you, it would've been standing till this day."
>
> Now, the last few days, the great roaring and popping. Then, here come out a paper of science, said, "It's all honeycombed; it's got to go under." They just know it. And you watch, the water will come plumb back into the Salton Sea. Los Angeles is doomed for judgment. I tell you before it happened, that you might know when it does happen. I never spoke that by myself. And I've never had Him to tell me one thing but what happened. And you can bear record of that. That's right. When? I don't know. I went out, and they told me what I said. And I listened, went back and searched the Scripture. You know, Jesus said, almost in them same words about Capernaum; and Sodom and Gomorrah was in the bottom of the Dead Sea, I suppose was then. And later, about a hundred years later, Capernaum slid into the sea, and it's in the sea. The same God that put Sodom in the sea for its sins, the same God that put Capernaum in the sea for its sins, the same God will put Los Angeles in the sea for its sins, that city of corruption ("Works Is Faith Expressed," 61–64).[2]

Joe Brandt's dream, accompanied by the revelation vision by William Branham, reveals a very precise happening that is soon to take place. They both predict that part of California is going to be swallowed up into the Pacific Ocean. As authors, we do not want to predict a pandemonium on the West Coast; but it is "food for thought."

This reminds us of the words to the country song, sung by country legend George Strait. The song is "Ocean Front Property." Here are the lyrics to the chorus:

> I got some ocean front property in Arizona.
> From my front porch you can see the sea.
> I got some ocean front property in Arizona.
> If you'll buy that, I'll throw the golden gate in free.[3]

Of course George Strait is not a prophet. But this would almost be humorous if it did not parallel what many prophets have predicted!

Endnotes

1. See www.biblebelievers.org.au/joebrandt.htm.
2. Ibid.
3. Dean Dillon, Hank Cochran, and Royce Porter, "Ocean Front Property," MCA, 1986.

Chapter 5

WILLIAM BRANHAM PROPHESIES A CALIFORNIA EARTHQUAKE

ONE OF THE foremost prophets in the last 75 years has been William Branham (April 6, 1909—December 24, 1965). To some, he was also controversial.

Branham claimed that from his early childhood he had supernatural experiences including prophetic visions. He said that in his early childhood, while assisting his father at a still, he heard a "Voice" that told him, "Don't you never drink, smoke, or defile your body in any way. There'll be a work for you to do when you get older."

Historians generally mark his 1946 meetings as inaugurating the modern healing revival. William Branham claimed to have received an angelic visitation on May 7, 1946, commissioning his worldwide ministry.

Although only 12 years old at the time, one co-author of this book actually experienced a live William Branham Healing Service in 1960. It was on the top floor of the Oral Roberts' Abundant Life Building on South Boulder Avenue in Tulsa, Oklahoma. He was greatly impressed with the extreme anointing and bona fide miracles that occurred.

In doing research for this book on earthquakes and the end-times, it was an honor to communicate with Rev. Pearry Green, who has carried the torch of the William Branham Ministries. In his book, *The Acts of the Prophet,* Rev. Pearry Green spoke at some length of William Branham's prophetic words regarding earthquakes in the end times:[1]

EARTHQUAKE JUDGMENT

In 1964, Brother Branham's ministry reached into the literal shaking of the earth. He and several other brothers had again gathered to hunt javelina. The locale was the area we often refer to as "Sunset," which is in the general vicinity of Klondike, Arizona. This is the same general area as where the angels descended. Because of the memory of that event the year before, one might have expected other outstanding events to emanate from this spot—yet as Brother Branham and a close friend, Brother Banks Wood, returned to camp, there was no hint of anything unusual. We know now that, at that very moment, megatons of rock must have lain poised for movement deep in the bowels of the earth.

As Brother Branham and Brother Wood walked along that day, the Spirit of the Lord spoke to Brother Branham and told him to pick up a stone and cast it into the air. Obediently, he did as he was told. As the stone struck the earth, a small whirlwind came down with it, and he simply spoke the words, "Thus saith the Lord." He turned to Brother Wood and said, "You watch, there will be something happen. You must do something to cause things to happen. This is the way that things are started."

Around 10:00 the next morning, the hunting party was preparing to break camp and the members of the party were engaged in various activities such as preparing their game, taking down their tents, and loading the trucks. Being a conservationist, Brother Branham was careful to leave the campground clean and to ensure that the campfire was completely out, thus he shoveled dirt onto it.

Brother Roy Roberson, a veteran of World War II, was standing nearby. Brother Branham put his hand on Brother Roy's shoulder and told him to quickly take cover because something was about to happen. Then Brother Branham walked away from the brothers, because he knew it would come to where he was.

One of the brothers was taking motion pictures of Brother Branham at the time and just as his camera ran out of film, over the bluff from the north a whirlwind came down a few feet above Brother Branham's head. The violent force of this whirlwind was so great that it cut part of the bluff out; it threw three-cornered rocks for over 100 yards (many of the rocks were the size of a man's fist); it cut off the tops off the mesquite trees; and the sound of its fury filled the air.

Naturally the brothers who were with him took cover. Some dove under the trucks or scrambled beneath the bushes, but Brother Branham stood still. The whirlwind went back up like a funnel, clapped like a great thunder, whirled around again, and came back down. This happened three times. Brother Branham simply took off his hat and looked up into the midst of this whirlwind as it came down right over his head.

When it lifted the last time, it went back the same direction that it came. Brother Branham put his hat back on his head and reminded the brothers that God spoke to Job in a whirlwind (Job 38:1). After the Lord gave him permission to tell them, Brother Branham explained that it was a judgment sign and that it spoke in three great blasts. The men only heard the blasting, but Brother Branham understood what was said, "Judgment striking West Coast." Indeed, the whirlwind had left in the northwesterly direction, toward the West Coast of America.

Before we learn of the extent of this impending judgment, let us return to a few years prior to when this prophet of God first spoke of such things. We must remember that God not only sends prophets for the edification of the people of God, but He also sends them to pronounce judgment upon those who will not listen. To the one, the words of the prophet bring life; to the other they bring death and destruction.

The first mention of earthquake judgment by Brother Branham was about 1935 when he said that the time would come that the sea would weep its way into the desert.

On May 2, 1951, as he spoke his sermon entitled "The Angel of the Lord" to a congregation in Los Angeles, California, he warned that judgment was approaching. "Over on the East Coast, they're always hollering to me, 'Why you going to the West Coast?' 'Everybody pulls out to Los Angeles.' Maybe that's God's place; that's right. Right here is probably where judgment will strike. And that's right. Let's get ready. My, this will probably be the first place it'll be hit, right in here. O Church, hold to God's unchanging hand. Pray."

In Chicago, Illinois, in a sermon entitled "The Great Coming Revival" preached in the afternoon of July 18, 1954, he admonished, "This great city here, which has become wicked like the rest of the world, one of these days you won't receive mercy; you've got to receive judgment. And while God's hand is... moving in mercy and the doors are open, run into [it] and be safe, into the Lord Jesus Christ. It's a sign. Look out on the West Coast, up in the Puget Sound. Here recently, how those big tidal waves struck. Never been known in the world to ever do that—how those signs, earthquakes, perplexed of times, distress between nations. Look at it today."

Jesus spoke of these signs. "And there shall be signs in the sun, and in the moon, and in the stars; and upon the earth distress of nations, with perplexity; the sea and the waves roaring; Men's hearts failing them for fear, and for looking after those things which are coming on the earth: for the powers of heaven shall be shaken. And then shall they see the Son of man coming in a cloud with power and great glory. And when these things begin to come to pass, then look up, and lift up your heads; for your redemption draweth nigh." (Luke 21:25–28).

In a sermon entitled "The Second Coming of the Lord," preached on April 17, 1957, Brother Branham again warned of impending judgment. "The other day, over in California, up in Oakland...it was the first time that my wife had ever been in an earthquake. I was sitting in the barbershop, and I—the room shook just a little. And the radio quickly announced an earthquake was on, said, 'They're looking for another one in about eight minutes.' And I thought, 'Oh, what if this is the last one!'" At that time, not many people perceived that a prophet of God was fulfilling Scripture by referring to the last earthquake.

As Brother Branham continued, he warned, "That is the finger of Almighty God, saying, 'The handwriting's on the wall.' Brethren, it's later than you think. Sodom and Gomorrah little knew, that night, that they were living their last hour. Little did Egypt know that the death angel that had been predicted to come would come that night. Little did Pearl Harbor realize that raid that took place. We are weighed in the balance and found wanting (Daniel 5). We are near the end time."

The whirlwind descended three times on that day in 1964, as Brother Branham stood near the campsite at Sunset. The first time judgment struck the West Coast was shortly thereafter, on Good Friday, March 27, 1964, in the form of an earthquake in Alaska in which a large area of land slipped toward the sea up to 66 feet, according to the United States Geological Survey (USGS). This earthquake is the second largest that the world has known in recent history,[1] having a moment magnitude[2] measuring 9.2.

In a sermon entitled "Identified Christ of All Ages," preached on April 9, 1964, Brother Branham explained, "The first time the earthquake ever shook the whole earth was on Good Friday. The last time it shook it was another Good Friday. What did it shake for? Because they had rejected their Messiah. Why did it shake again? They've done the same thing. See? Laodicea church age, any scholar knows that He was on the outside knocking, try—'Lo, I stand at the door and knock.' The only church age that ever completely put Him out" (Revelation 3:14–22).

A similarity of these two Good Fridays was published in the July 1964 issue of the National Geographic magazine. Their article concerning the Good Friday earthquake in Alaska began, "'And, behold…the earth did quake, and the rocks rent.' St. Matthews's account of the first Good Friday saw fearful repetition almost 2,000 years later when, on March 27, 1964, the earth again strained its thin coat and burst its seams, spewing sudden destruction."[3]

On December 27, 1964, in his message "Who Do You Say This Is?" Brother Branham again gave warning,

"Look at the earthquakes over here in California. I predict, before the coming of the Lord Jesus that God will sink that place. I believe that Hollywood and Los Angeles and them [sic] filthy places over there, that God Almighty will sink them. They'll go beneath the bottom of the sea."

Though many of us followed his message and believed him to be the prophet of God to this generation, yet even at that hour, we did not perceive the prediction of judgment upon the West Coast of America.

Again on Good Friday, one year later, April 16, 1965, Alaska experienced another quake. Though less severe than the previous year, it still had a 5.9 magnitude.

Brother Branham preached a series of meetings in Los Angeles, California, from April 24 to 29, 1965. In the sermon entitled "Proving His Word," preached April 26, 1965, he exhorted the people, saying, "Surely, if God gives a fish and a bird discernment, how much more should He give His children[?] We know that we're at the end time and judgment is waiting, so let's be real reverent. Flee to God with all your heart. 'O Capernaum, thou who art exalted into heaven, will be brought down into hell,' and today she lays beneath the bed of the waters."

Prior to Brother Branham's preaching in the Biltmore Hotel in Los Angeles, California, the evening of April 29, 1965, a very dear friend, Sister Florence Shakarian, sang a song under the anointing, which was characteristic of her singing. Sister Florence had been sick for a long time. A few months prior to this, Brother Demos Shakarian had asked Brother Branham to pray for his sister, who was dying of cancer. At that time Brother Branham was given a word from the Lord concerning Sister Florence. He told Brother Demos that she would not die then, but she would die sometime between 2:00 and 3:00 some morning; he had seen her lying in state in a vision.

Sister Florence's anointed song that night was a tremendous blessing and the congregation was deeply moved. At the end of her song, Brother Branham, sitting on the platform next to Brother Carl Williams, nudged Brother Carl and said, "Do you hear that?" Brother Carl asked him what he meant, and Brother Branham replied, "She's walking up the Golden Stairs, can't you hear her?"

At about this same time, a man rose up and brought one of those powerful, spine-tingling messages in tongues that are often given in Pentecostal congregations. You could almost feel the anointing from the words this man brought—so forceful and with such authority was it given. The interpretation came immediately from the other side of the auditorium and said words similar to this, "Oh daughter of Zion, thou shalt not fear, thou shalt not worry, for thou shalt live to see the coming of the Lord."

Brother Billy Paul, who was in the audience that day, was deeply disturbed by this. The message had come with such force and such anointing, yet he knew this message contradicted what Brother Branham had received from the Lord. No explanation was forthcoming at this time and Brother Branham went on to deliver his message, "Choosing of a Bride" [April 29, 1965 p.m.].

Earlier that morning of April 29, 1965, a magnitude 6.5 earthquake took place just down the coast from Alaska, centering in the Puget Sound, 15 miles south of Seattle, Washington. Concerned by the many recent earthquakes, people asked Brother Branham if he thought it would continue to come their way.

As Brother Branham began his sermon, he addressed their questions. "That great monster laying up yonder that flipped hisself [sic] over in Alaska a few days ago, threw its tail up again this morning along about down around Washington. He could head this way mighty easy. And if the Holy Spirit ever tells me definitely—Some of you has [sic] been…asking me that. 'Is it going to happen here, Brother Branham?' No, I don't know that. I just don't know, and till I do know—That's the truth. I always wanted to be honest with you. I'm just not going to presume, take any ideas, or some—what I believe, or something like that. When I tell you, it's going to be—Well, He's got to tell me first, and then I'll tell you.…If I tell you anything in the name of the Lord, it's truly that that's who told me that." At the end of the sermon, their question was answered.

As Brother Branham concluded his sermon that evening, he prophesied, "You don't know what time that this city one day is going to be laying out here in the bottom of this ocean. 'O, Capernaum,' said Jesus, 'thou who exalted into heaven will be brought down into hell: for if the mighty works had been done in Sodom and Gomorrah, it would have been standing till this day' (Matthew 11:23; Luke 10:15). And Sodom and Gomorrah lays at the bottom of the Dead Sea, and Capernaum is in the bottom of the sea. Thou city who claims to be the city of the angels, who has exalted yourself into heaven and sent all the dirty, filthy things of fashions and things, till even the foreign countries come here to pick up our filth and send it away, with your fine churches and steeples, and so forth the way you do—remember, one day you will be laying in the bottom of this sea! You're great honeycomb under you right now. The wrath of God is belching right beneath you. How much longer He will hold this sandbar hanging over that, when that ocean out yonder a mile deep will slide in there plumb back to the Salton Sea. It will be worse than the last day of Pompeii. Repent, Los Angeles! Repent the rest of you and turn to God! The hour of His wrath is upon the earth. Flee while there is time to flee and come into Christ. Let us pray."

Let's look at three of the places mentioned in this prophecy. Los Angeles, located on the West Coast of America, is a coastal city bordering the Pacific Ocean. The Salton Sea is located approximately 135 miles southeast of Los Angeles, and it is approximately 80 miles from the Pacific Ocean. Pompeii was an ancient city in Italy, located on the coast of the Mediterranean Sea. It was inhabited by many wealthy landowners and prosperous merchants and manufacturers. In 79 A.D., Mount Vesuvius, the nearby volcano, erupted and buried Pompeii beneath lava and ash. History shows that the occupants of that city did not heed the signs of an impending disaster. Instead, they continued on with their daily lives, rebuilding and repairing previous earthquake damages.

After Brother Branham finished praying, he continued admonishing and warning, saying, "It's a solemn moment. I don't know how to express it. I've tried to leave the pulpit three or four times, and I can't do it. This is a solemn hour. Don't you never [sic] forget it.... Look at the nominal churches coming in. When the sleeping virgin come [sic] for oil, she failed to get it. The Bride went in. The rapture went up. While they went to buy oil, the Bridegroom come [sic]. Are you asleep? Wake up quickly, and come to yourself, and let us pray each one like we were dying at this minute, in the name of the Lord. Let's each one pray in your own way. God Almighty, have mercy upon us, Lord. Have mercy on me. Have mercy upon us all. What good does it do, no matter what we do, if we fail in these things[?] I stand and ask for mercy, O God, before this great city sinks beneath the sea and judgments of God sweep this coast; I pray, God, that You'll call Your Bride. I commit them to You now in the name of Jesus Christ. Amen."

This was a great moment for those of us who believed that Brother Branham was the prophet of God with the spirit of Elijah, when the realization swept over us that the sermon we had just heard, and what we had heard this great man of God say in other sermons, all pointed to a tremendous prophecy of doom for the West Coast. Now we realized that he was prophesying. Knowing him to be a Word prophet (someone that the Word prophesied would come), we knew that he spoke nothing unless it could be found in the Scriptures.

In his morning sermon on July 18, 1965, "Trying to Do God a Service without Being the Will of God," Brother Branham spoke about America, "I don't even pray for it. How can I pray for it, and it won't repent under the mighty powers of God demonstrated before it, and denying, and closing the doors to it, and walking away? I commit it to God. And she's going further away, and now she's going to sink. Just watch what happens. Nearly one-tenth of the earth is ready to fall in. Science says that."

As he preached his morning sermon on July 25, 1965, "Anointed Ones at the End Time," Brother Branham said, "But we've been told by the Lord Jesus that when these things that we see now begin to come to pass, then to lift up our heads for our redemption is drawing nigh (Luke 21:28). Now, what 'drawing nigh' means, I do not know. May mean, as the scientist said the other day on the television, speaking of the great thousands of miles break in the earth that's going to sink. He was asked the question, 'It could sink there (that's Los Angeles, the West Coast)?' And many of you seen [sic] how they followed it with radar, and went up through—broke in below San Jose, went across over into Alaska, out through the Aleutian Islands, about 200 miles out into the sea, and come back down into San Diego, went around in behind Los Angeles and come up there, a great pocket. And all these earthquakes we've been having is [sic] the volcanic hitting this great hollow dipper like, in there. I can't call the name that they called it. However, when that shakes, that gives these earthquakes we've been having for years on the West Coast. Now, it's cracked all the way around."

That night, he preached "What Is the Attraction on the Mountain?" and he spoke of the prophecy of the splitting of the Mount of Olives by an earthquake and the earthquake to the Gentiles in the last day, saying, "Listen close now. This is 'thus saith the Lord.' It's the Scriptures." At this, he referred to Zechariah who prophesied of the coming of Christ in the last days. Zechariah 14:4–5, "And his feet shall stand in that day upon the mount of Olives, which is before Jerusalem on the east, and the mount of Olives shall cleave in the midst thereof toward the east and toward the west, and there shall be a very great valley; and half of the mountain shall remove toward the north, and half of it toward the south. And ye shall flee to the valley of the mountains; for the valley of the mountains shall reach unto Azal: yea, ye shall flee, like as ye fled from before the earthquake in the days of Uzziah king of Judah—"

He continued, "Another earthquake splitting open the earth! If you want to follow out a Scripture here, notice in this fifth verse, it applies that the cleaving of the Mount of Olives is due to an earthquake, and this is confirmed by Isaiah 29:6—" "Thou shalt be visited of the Lord of hosts with thunder, and with earthquake, and great noise, with storm and tempest, and the flame of devouring fire." And Revelation 16:17–18, "And the seventh angel poured out his vial into the air; and there came a great voice out of the temple of heaven, from the throne, saying, It is done. And there were voices, and thunders, and lightnings; and there was a great earthquake, such as was not since men were upon the earth, so mighty an earthquake, and so great."

He continued, "Exactly! What is it? The same prophet told of His first coming, seen [sic] His second coming! Notice, 'As in the days of the earthquake—' See what the earthquakes are doing? See the predictions of them?....See where we're at? 'Nations are breaking, Israel's awakening, the signs that our prophets foretold'—that earthquake to the Gentiles to the last day."

In his evening sermon, "A Thinking Man's Filter," preached on August 22, 1965, Brother Branham, spoke on a coast-to-coast and border-to-border telephone hookup and clearly pronounced judgment upon America, speaking of a large chunk of land that will sink and the effects of it. "The Holy Spirit in my own heart tonight cries, 'Blind Laodicea, how oft God would've give [sic] you a revival, but now your time has come. It's too late now. How did you laugh and make fun of the people that God sent to you? But now your time has come. Oh, United States, United States, how that God would've hovered [over] you as a hen does its brood, but you would not.' Now, this voice is going from coast to coast, from north to south, and east to west. How God would've hovered [over] you, but you would not. Now your time has come. Nations are breaking; the world is falling apart. Fifteen hundred mile chunk of it, three or four hundred miles wide, will sink hundred—or maybe 40 miles down into that great fault out yonder one of these days, and waves will shoot plumb out to the state of Kentucky. And when it does, it'll shake the world so hard that everything on top of it will shake down!"

Notice how Brother Branham said, "Oh, United States, United States, how that God would've hovered [over] you as a hen does its brood, but you would not," just as Jesus Christ said, "O Jerusalem, Jerusalem, thou that killest the prophets, and stonest them which are sent unto thee, how often would I have gathered thy children together, even as a hen gathereth her chickens under her wings, and ye would not!" (Matthew 23:37) If the United States and the people who call themselves the people of God, that say they have the baptism of the Holy Ghost, that say they are Spirit-filled, and that believe in the gifts of the Spirit and divine healing, had only known their day when God visited this generation in the life of a prophet!

Speaking to the Lord in prayer in a sermon entitled "Thirst," preached on September 19, 1965, Brother

Branham confessed, "We realize that judgment is striking. Great faults are falling in, and the nation is shaking, and earthquakes in divers places. Great historical things that we've heard of in the days past of judgment, through the Bible, and we see it repeating again today. The prophecy saying, 'As it was in the days of Noah, so shall it be in the coming of the Son of man. As it was in the days of Lot, so shall it be in the coming of the Son of man' (Luke 17:26–30), and we see it happening now. Man's hearts failing; perplexity of time; distress between nations (Luke 21:25–26). God, we know we're at the end time."

Why do I include all these direct quotations from Brother Branham's sermons? It is simply because I wish to clarify what he actually said in the face of much that is attributed to him that he did not say. Remember, he never set dates. He never said when it would happen, except that he predicted that it would happen before the coming of the Lord.

In a sermon entitled "The Rapture" preached on December 4, 1965, in Yuma, Arizona, he reminded the people of the prophecy for the West Coast. "I remember just my last message in California where I thought I'd never go back again, when I predicted Los Angeles will go beneath the ocean. And thus saith the Lord, it will. She's done; she's washed; she's finished. What hour? I don't know when, but it will be sunk."

On December 6, 1965, in San Bernardino, California, as he preached the sermon "Modern Events Are Made Clear by Prophecy," Brother Branham made this statement as he [sang] this song, "'Nations are breaking, Israel's awakening, the signs that the prophets foretold. The Gentile days numbered, with horrors encumbered, (Watch her slide into the sea!) return, O dispersed, to your own. The day of redemption is near. Man's hearts are failing for fear. Be filled with the Spirit, have your lamps trimmed and clear. Look up! Your redemption is near.' Brother, sister, it's a scary time. Watch the things [that are] prophesied; watch the things happen. Watch all the prophecy being fulfilled; then we see what all this is about. It's not a bunch, a streak of fanaticism. It's God confirming His Words exactly. Exactly. The Rock (I Corinthians 10:4) is smitten, friends, flee to It as quick as you can. Prophecy is vindicating the day that we're living in."

Brother Branham was approached by the various brothers who lived in California, asking him what they should do. While on a hunting trip he said to one group, "People will make fun of the destruction of the earthquake that we have said would happen, 'thus saith the Lord,' on the West Coast of America, but I want you brothers to know this, that if you have any friends or relation in Los Angeles, if I were you, I'd get them out as quickly as possible." Then he told the story of how the angel of the Lord had told him that his wife, Sister Meda, would give birth to a little boy and that he would name him Joseph. He said, "The same angel of the Lord that told me that I would have Joseph by Meda told me that Los Angeles would sink and slide into the Pacific Ocean as the result of an earthquake."

Let's return now to the state of unrest in which Brother Billy Paul found himself concerning the conflicting prophecy over Sister Florence Shakarian when the message in tongues had gone forth on April 29, 1965.

According to Brother Billy's testimony, as Brother Branham and Billy were walking back to their hotel,

Brother Branham perceived that something was troubling Billy and he said, "Paul, what's wrong?"

"Oh, nothing Dad," Billy replied.

After a few steps, Brother Branham asked again, "What's troubling you, Paul?"

"Well, Daddy," said Billy, "You heard that message of tongues and interpretation there."

"So what?" replied Brother Branham.

"But Dad, you know that you said that the angel of the Lord told you that she would die between 2:00 and 3:00 in the morning."

Notice Brother Branham's reply—so typical of him—he answers and yet does not speak against the tongues and interpretation. "Well, all I can say is, Paul, that the Lord has not told me any different."

The morning of September 11, 1965, Brother Branham was at the Ramada Inn in Phoenix, Arizona, about to preach a sermon entitled "God's Power to Transform." It was at this time that I witnessed the answer to the question troubling Brother Billy Paul. I was doing the telephone hookup. Brother Carl Williams and Brother Branham were sitting at the head table when I received a phone call from Brother Richard Shakarian, who informed me that his aunt, Sister Florence, had died during the night. I walked over and told Brother Branham and Brother Carl. Brother Branham asked me to find out when she died, so I went back and phoned Brother Richard, who told me that she had died at 2:45 that morning. I then went back and told Brother Branham, who replied, "That's exactly what the vision said."

I will leave it up to you to decide whether the tongues and interpretation were of God, or whether it was from someone's zealousness of an anointing that was not "thus saith the Lord." The angel of God had told the prophet of God that she would die between 2:00 and 3:00 in the morning. She died at 2:45 in the morning. The message in tongues and interpretation said she would not die, but our sister does sleep in Christ. It happened exactly when the angel of the Lord said that it would.

Though the evidence overwhelmingly points to Brother Branham being the prophet of God for this age, yet there are those who tread critical and dangerous pathways. In the matter of the prophesied destruction of the West Coast, their unbelief causes them to scoff against the very warning that God has given this generation.

For example, some claimed Brother Branham predicted the destruction of Los Angeles would occur before another international convention of the Full Gospel Business Men could be held in that city. Some laugh and scorn, saying that the 1968 convention was held in Los Angeles. I challenge this claim—first of all on the basis that I do not believe Brother Branham made the statement. The man who claimed he had it on tape would not permit me to hear the tape. His claim is that Brother Branham did not make the statement publicly, but whispered it to someone next to him on the platform and that his microphone picked up Brother Branham's voice. Strangely enough, the man will not allow any of us to hear this whisper attributed to Brother Branham. Secondly, the 1968 Full Gospel Business Men convention was held in the Beverly Hills Hilton Hotel, in Beverly Hills, California, not Los Angeles. For their sakes, I would not like to see them schedule one in Los Angeles if the prophet of God did make this statement. For myself, I wait for that day because I believe it is the day that shall bring forth the resurrection of those who sleep in Christ Jesus.

One world-renowned denominational Pentecostal leader made fun in a letter saying, "No wonder that God had to take William Branham off the scene. Anybody that would predict the destruction of Los Angeles—with 420,000 Holy Ghost filled believers in the city—God would certainly condemn a man for making such a judgment." This man is ignorant of the Scriptures and of the move of God that has taken place in this day. His action was childish, the reflection of an immature judgment and understanding. I won't name him, but I sincerely hope that he reads this book because he must be made to understand that he needs to repent. He also went on to say, "William Branham spoke about having an angel of God with him all the time. That angel must have been taking his Christmas vacation on the night of December 18, 1965." To me this is blaspheming. It is making fun of the Spirit of God. In love I say that I hope he repents and retracts these words, lest he face them on Judgment Day. He does not understand that God at one time killed 70,000 men in one day simply because one man sinned among the children of Israel (II Samuel 24:15). This is the God of the Bible, not the God of men's imaginations.

There is another internationally-known evangelist who wrote in his paper concerning these predictions of earthquakes that he did not find such things in the Scripture and that he believed that these were just occurrences which would continue, but which have absolutely no significance to the people of God. This man also proves himself ignorant of the Scriptures, because he does not recall Daniel 12:1. "And at that time shall Michael stand up, the great prince which standeth for the children of thy people: and there shall be a time of trouble, such as never was since there was a nation even to that same time: and at that time thy people shall be delivered, every one that shall be found written in the book."

He must have been ignorant of Revelation 6:12–14 which states that at the opening of the Sixth Seal there shall be a great earthquake. "And I beheld when he had opened the sixth seal, and, lo, there was a great earthquake; and the sun became black as sackcloth of hair, and the moon became as blood. And the stars of heaven fell unto the earth, even as a fig tree casteth her untimely figs, when she is shaken of a mighty wind. And the heaven departed as a scroll when it is rolled together; and every mountain and island were moved out of their places." In the series Brother Branham preached March 17–24, 1963, on "The Revelation of the Seven Seals," one can see that the Sixth Seal happens to the Jews when Christ reveals Himself to His brethren, but the Gentile Bride has been taken away.

The earthquake becomes, then, a pivotal point around which the words of the prophet sweep in telling the Bride to come out and make herself ready, that same Bride will see that what delivered the people of God would also bring judgment upon the ungodly.

On one occasion I was reading to Brother Branham from chapter 14 in the book of Revelation on through the 18th chapter. Revelation 18:4 reads, "And I heard another voice from heaven, saying, Come out of her, my people, that ye be not partakers of her sins, and that ye receive not of her plagues." As I read these words, the realization struck me that this was Brother Branham's message. It was him that said, "Come out of her," speaking of coming out of the systems, the denominations, the Roman plague, the daughters of the harlot, and everything else that would blind the eyes. Then, I knew that he not only fulfilled Malachi 4, Luke 17:30, and Revelation 10:7, but he was also fulfilling the 18th chapter of the book of Revelation.

As I read Revelation 18:8–10, which speaks of this great city Babylon, that sits on seven hills (Revelation 17:9), Brother Branham [interjected] a comment.

"Therefore shall her plagues come in one day, death, and mourning, and famine; and she shall be utterly burned with fire: for strong is the Lord God who judgeth her. And the kings of the earth, who have committed fornication and lived deliciously with her, shall bewail her, and lament for her, when they shall see the smoke of her burning, Standing afar off for the fear of her torment—"

When I read this, Brother Branham said, "Atomic power."

"—saying, Alas, alas, that great city Babylon, that mighty city! for in one hour is thy judgment come."

If this were ordinary fire, they would try to put it out. Brother Branham on May 13, 1954, in the sermon "The Mark of the Beast," said, "I say this as God's prophet: The Russian empire will drop an atomic bomb of some sort on the Vatican City and destroy it in one hour. Thus saith the Lord." Here it is in the Scriptures, proving it to be so. A prophet of God had to stand on this earth and say, "Thus saith the Lord," in order that it might fulfill the Scripture. Likewise he had to stand on the earth and say, "Thus saith the

Lord," California will sink, in order that it would sink. The word of the Lord has to be spoken before God will bring it to pass.

Revelation 18:20 says, "Rejoice over her, thou heaven, and ye holy apostles, and prophets; for God hath avenged you on her." God is saying, "Rejoice, I have avenged you of the Roman system. It's gone. It's destroyed by fire."

I continued reading aloud to Brother Branham, and after I read verse 21 of Revelation 18, "And a mighty angel took up a stone like a great millstone, and cast it into the sea, saying, Thus with violence shall that great city Babylon be thrown down, and shall be found no more at all," Brother Branham made this statement, "Notice, Brother Green, the two Babylons." This was in August 1964, which was before the prophecy of the destruction of Los Angeles was given in April 1965. Therefore, at that time, I did not perceive what he meant by "two Babylons"—one being destroyed by fire and one being cast into the ocean.

Notice the Scripture that he said would happen to Los Angeles, "And the voice of harpers, and musicians, and of pipers, and trumpeters, shall be heard no more at all in thee; and no craftsman, of whatsoever craft he be, shall be found any more in thee; and the sound of a millstone shall be heard no more at all in thee; And the light of a candle shall shine no more at all in thee; and the voice of the bridegroom and of the bride shall be heard no more at all in thee; for thy merchants were the great men of the earth; for by thy sorceries were all nations deceived" (Revelation 18:22–23) You cannot light a candle underwater.

Return now to that day when Brother Branham turned to Brother Billy Paul and said about Sister Florence Shakarian, "Billy, all I can say is that God has told me no different." Brother Billy Paul testified that after making this statement, Brother Branham turned to him and said, "Billy, where are you standing?"

"Downtown Los Angeles," Billy Paul replied.

"Where are you standing?"

"In front of the May Company, downtown Los Angeles," replied Billy.

"Billy," he said, "I may not be here, but you won't be an old man until sharks will swim right where we are standing."

Brother Branham preached his last message in California on December 7, 1965, in Covina. In this message, "Leadership," he reminded and warned the people, "Look here. Do you know what the Lord says about Los Angeles and these places here? She's gone. You remember what I told you about two years ago, how that earthquake would come in Canada, up here in Alaska? I also [told] you that 'Hollywood and Los Angeles is sliding into the ocean. California, you're doomed—not only California, but you, world, you're doomed. Church, unless you get right with God, you're doomed.' Thus saith the Holy Spirit. Have you ever heard me use that name unless it come to pass? Ask you. You've known me 20 years. Did I ever tell you anything in the name of the Lord but what come to pass? If everything I've ever told you would happen, happened, say, 'Amen.' (The congregation answered, 'Amen.') See? I tell you, now is the hour, you better be getting right, all of us."

That night when he finished this sermon on "Leadership," he did something that none of us who followed him closely had ever seen him do before. That night in Covina, California, he closed his portion of the service with the song "Till We Meet." "Till we meet, till we meet, at Jesus' feet..." I was sitting at the head table with Brother Carl Williams. I saw as Brother Branham walked off the edge of the platform with Brother Billy Paul, he pulled away from Brother Billy, stepped back on the platform, and while they sang the song, he waved good-bye. This is something that I had never seen him do before. As I witnessed this, I nudged Brother Carl Williams and said, "Brother Carl, is he telling California goodbye?"—This was his last visit to California.

There are those people who have said, "I will move off the West Coast when God tells me to." Without a shadow of a doubt, God has already told you to. You were told when God sent a prophet to this generation who said, "Thus saith the Lord, the city of Los Angeles, as the result of an earthquake, will break off and slide off into the Pacific Ocean." If you are a spiritual person and believe that this man was the fulfillment of Malachi 4, a forerunner of the second coming of the Lord Jesus Christ, and you live on the West Coast, you will get out as quickly as possible, for God has indeed spoken.

1. "Largest Earthquakes in the World Since 1900." U.S. Geological Survey. April 11, 2012. Web. Retrieved September 5, 2014. www.earthquake.usgs.gov.

2. For the quakes above 6.5, the moment magnitude is often used instead of the Richter scale.

3. "Alaska Earthquake: Horror Strikes on Good Friday." *National Geographic magazine.* July 1964. Vol. 126. No. 1, 112.

William Branham was certainly one of the foremost healing evangelists and prophets of his generation, by the time he died in 1965. Numerous prophecies have been fulfilled that he foretold. However, he is not without his critics.

We trust that his prophecy about an atomic bomb being dropped on the Vatican does not alarm people, especially Catholics. We have also been in downtown Los Angeles in front of the May Company department store. Brother Branham's prophecy that sharks would be swimming in front of that store is certainly frightening and disturbing.

We strive only to present you with credible prophecies that have been given regarding earthquakes in the end times. It is up to you, the reader, to sort out these various prophecies as they line up with the Holy Scripture.

ENDNOTE

1. Pearry Green, *The Acts of the Prophet* (Tucson, AZ: Tucson Tabernacle, 1993). See also http://www.tucsontabernacle.org/eq-facts-list/1376-eq-judgmt-acts-of-prophet.

Chapter 6

NITA JOHNSON'S PROPHETIC VISION: JUDGMENT OF ALL OF AMERICA

NITA JOHNSON, A well-respected current-day prophetess, "is the president and founder of the World for Jesus Ministries, Inc., a ministry established to reach the world with the love of Jesus."[1]

On January 27, 1989, a prophetic vision was given to Nita Johnson. In the following excerpt, the editor's notes appear in brackets.

> I was awakened in the middle of the night. The Lord said to me, "Why do you think I gave you that vision of the United States?" I replied, "I don't know, Lord, why did you?" He then responded, "A surrogate mother won't work. Sarah could not be one to Ishmael. It's not My way." As I was pondering what that could possibly mean, He followed with, "Only what is born of faith can work."
>
> While the Lord gave birth to America's liberty and planted in her bosom a hope, He promised to be her protective covering if she would meet His conditions. He did not give birth to this sinful and rebellious nation. Although He has given birth to His church, a nation within a nation, He did not give birth to this antagonistic entity we call America. It was the blood, sweat and tears of man that gave it birth. Humanists swam in the womb with this nation and humanists have helped give it birth. They have nurtured it, coddled it and flaunted it as the son of their pride.

On the other hand, it was the church who fought for the right of motherhood. She fought for the right to set up the rules and even discipline the spoiled child when it was bad. But she, alas, has only been "the surrogate mother for a rebellious Ishmael."

It was Sarah who wisely declared at last, "Cast out this bondwoman and her son, for the son of this bondwoman shall not be heir with my son!" However, while this is true, Abraham suffered over releasing Ishmael and sending him away. Even so, our Eternal Father suffers over the future of the people of America. He must cast away the rebellious but He does it with great pain. What America as a nation doesn't understand is that we have been reaping the benefits of the churches inheritance for over two hundred years. While the church has not been the model bride any more than Sarah had been a perfect wife, we the Church are, nonetheless, God's bride and the spiritual nation of Israel. So while the Lord loves His "spiritual Israel" (the church) and although He must even chastise His elect, He will cast out the irreverent Ishmael (The United States). Though God loves man, He hates sin and will cast out from the inheritance those that choose to serve sin. For these it might be said; He has little regard. May we also remember it was not God who first rejected America. Although He has stretched His arms out to us, we are the ones who have refused Him. So, fear not, Church, that which is born of Earth will stand. God has in His judgment remembered mercy. What I'm about to share is the way in which God is going to, in effect, cast out this rebellious America [He] calls Ishmael. The process will begin while the church is still here. In fact, it has already begun and will continue until all is fully executed. I want to add one more thing before I share the vision the Bible tells us:

And if you say in your [minds and] hearts, How shall we know which words the Lord has not spoken? When a prophet speaks in the name of the Lord, if the word does not come to pass or prove true, that is a word which the Lord has not spoken. The prophet has spoken it presumptuously; you shall not be afraid of him" (Deut. 18:21–22). So we are to judge the word which is spoken in the Lord's name by waiting to see if it comes to pass. If it does, we need to believe it and respond to God's warnings through it.

The Vision: On January 27, 1989, I had been in a spirit of prayer all night and was finally just starting to dose off to sleep. Suddenly, I was fully awakened by a vision of a map of the United States. It was not a vision in my head but was what some call an open vision out in front of me.

The map was in a silvery light and was completely sectioned off into states. Just as suddenly as it had appeared, I heard a voice, as robust as the sound of many waters yet with great intensity, begin to give directions. Starting with the West Coast, the voice would speak and that same silvery light would shoot down from the direction of heaven like a laser beam onto the map. The light would follow the path directed by the voice and then effects would follow as I will explain. First, the voice cried out—"The West Coast, California, Oregon and Washington, starting from the southern-most tip all the way up to Seattle, will suffer natural disasters, such as earthquakes, floods and fire, and enemy attack." The line shot up the map taking most of California and leaving only a small section that bordered on Arizona and Nevada. It went up through Oregon taking about half of that state and then on up through Washington, taking about one-third of that state, then out toward the ocean through Seattle. The minute the line touched Seattle, everything west of the line disappeared.

The voice then cried out, "Michigan, Indiana, Ohio, and Illinois will suffer natural disasters, such as floods, earthquakes and tornadoes, and enemy attack." Immediately, this line started at about where Lansing, Michigan, is and fanned down in what became two lines going south first. Then one line swung back up easterly through Ohio, going out over the Great Lake Erie through Cleveland. The other line swung down through Indiana and then headed back up northwesterly and went out into the Great Lake Michigan up by the way of the northeast corner of Illinois and out through Chicago. When it was done, it looked like two "u's," side-by-side. This affected areas all through the region, for instance, as far east as Detroit and easterly in Michigan to the Great Lake itself on the west. The whole southern part of the glove experienced cataclysmic results.

Next, the voice called out, "Most of Louisiana and all of Texas will suffer natural disasters, floods, hurricanes, tornadoes, and enemy attack." The line shot up through New Orleans east of Baton Rouge, up through Shreveport in a kind of wiggly way then cut off all of Texas. Texas disappeared. Louisiana experienced devastation but didn't disappear.

I was ready for this to end, yet the Lord continued. New York down through Pennsylvania, the Virginias, the eastern Part of Tennessee, Georgia, and Florida will suffer natural disasters of every kind, hurricanes, flooding, earthquakes, etc. and enemy attack. Then everything that was east of the line disappeared.

The Lord continued, "The Grand Canyon will suffer natural disasters." The line seemed to start at the bottom of the Grand Canyon heading northerly straight up to Montana through Yellowstone. This was also accompanied by cataclysmic disasters like floods, earthquakes, volcanoes, and fires. This affected a substantial area, including Arizona, Utah, western parts of Wyoming, the eastern tip of Idaho and southwestern part of Montana. The regions did not disappear, but experienced utter catastrophe.

Then Missouri, Mississippi, Arkansas, Alabama, West Tennessee, Kentucky, and on it went. There were severe heat waves, hailstorms, energy blackouts, severe snow and ice storms as well as extreme arctic cold spells to the loss of many lives. I saw it so often occur in some the least likely areas. Famines, pestilence, plagues, and more. Nevada and Utah were all but destroyed through natural disasters of every kind and ultimately enemy attack. They did, however, remain on the map. (Please note that I am not declaring that the states that disappeared fell off into the sea. I don't know why they disappeared, only that they did. Consequently, I am merely relating what I saw-not trying to interpret.) [Uninhabitable, or inhabited by invaders.]

I was so dumbstruck that I felt numb, even bruised. It was hard for me to pull it all together in my mind. I just sat there in shock. Finally, I realized if I didn't write it down, I'd lose a lot of it as there was so much detail. So I wrote what I could remember. Some states, such as New Mexico, were lost from my memory. I couldn't remember what happened to them, so I didn't record it.

I distinctly remember, however, that the only part of the U.S. that was not devastated was the Central United States, a region basically west of the Missouri River, as I have indicated on the map. I also realized that many of the things that would begin happening immediately would be of an unusual nature, such as natural disasters that would seem improbable or even impossible, at least for that particular geographical area.

I was instructed that this sequence of events would start immediately, picking up momentum with time until eventually the succession would be happening with gunshot rapidity, until all fulfilled. It's important to understand that the natural disasters did not specifically follow "the lines," but the lines seemed to indicate the borders of the severely affected areas. The only one exception was the line that went up through the Grand Canyon north to Montana. In that case, the line seemed to symbolize the central core of action with a radiating aftermath both to the east and west. I saw natural disasters in Alaska and the Hawaiian Islands followed by warheads.

Finally, I saw a severe diminishing of our nation's military. Officers, and enlisted men, as well as the closing of many critical bases were part of the scenario. [Authors' note: Many liken this to the severe military cuts under the Barack Obama administration!] Our ability to defend ourselves was critically reduced, to a point of near ineffectiveness. (The Military cut down was not incorporated in this vision, but was seen many years ago.)

> These disasters have already begun, just as He said they would. Since that vision, there have been two earthquakes in California, terrible fires, a hurricane on the East Coast that did what all the meteorologists said could never happen. The storm entered inland through Charleston, South Carolina, went north and headed back into the ocean through New York. Flooding for the first time in history was recorded in a community in northern Ohio resulting in unusual deaths. Most recently, there was an earthquake near the southern border of Missouri, and floods in the plains, and terrible disaster in Florida from tornados. Those are just a few instances, but hopefully, they're enough to drive the point home. These things are neither freak accidents, as some would have you believe, nor are they just satanic humor on mankind. Church, please realize that the Lord commanded everything that I saw hit the map. He also told me it was part of the sequential calamities which are warnings ultimately leading to full judgment assigned to this country. They are like blinking red lights along the path of judgment—Go back! Stop! Repent! The end is at hand! Will you hear? Will you pray? How in His great mercy would He gladly stop or minimize catastrophe for His praying church![2]

Nita Johnson's vision showed widespread devastation in the United States of America, especially for the state of California. However, her vision was also tempered with mercy.

The United States, en route to a true end-time judgment (as prophesied by Nita Johnson, with whom we totally agree), will experience widespread natural disasters of all kinds. These calamities are true warnings of divine judgment. As Nita Johnson rightfully concludes, the only hope is the praying church!

ENDNOTES

1. See http://www.worldforjesus.org/about-us.php.
2. See http://www.ubm1.org/?page=propheti.

Chapter 7

RECENT PROPHECIES

WE DON'T WANT to get carried away, interpreting events as more significant than they are. In this chapter, we are including several more recent prophecies made regarding earthquakes in these end times. We were fascinated to read the following, written by David Wilkerson in 1974, and quoted in a blog by Peter Kirk in March 2011—well before the recent earthquake in Japan.

> *The United States is going to experience in the not-too-distant future the most tragic earthquakes in its history. One day soon this nation will be reeling under the impact of the biggest news story of modern times. It will be coverage of the biggest most disastrous earthquake in history.*
>
> *It will cause widespread panic and fear. Without a doubt, it will become one of the most completely reported earthquakes ever. Television networks will suspend all programming and carry all day coverage.*
>
> *Another earthquake, possibly in Japan may precede the one that I see coming here. There is not the slightest doubt in my mind about this forthcoming massive earthquake in our continent.*
>
> *I am not at all convinced that this earthquake will take place in California. In fact, I believe it is going to take place where it is least expected. This terrible earthquake may happen in an area that not known as an earthquake belt. It will be so high on*

the Richter scale that it will trigger two other major earthquakes....

For ten years I have been warning about a thousand fires coming to New York City. It will engulf the whole megaplex, including areas of New Jersey and Connecticut. Major cities all across America will experience riots and blazing fires—such as we saw in Watts, Los Angeles, years ago.

There will be riots and fires in cities worldwide. There will be looting—including Times Square, New York City. What we are experiencing now is not a recession, not even a depression. We are under God's wrath....

How should we react to such prophecies? In the past on this blog I [Peter Kirk] have discussed modern day prophecies by Smith Wigglesworth and Sharon Stone. On my understanding, the gift of prophecy today is not primarily about predicting future events. However, I believe that on occasions God does reveal the future to his people, not to satisfy their curiosity, but as warnings and to demonstrate that he is in control of events.

Surely the Sovereign LORD does nothing without revealing his plan to his servant the prophets.

—AMOS 3:7 (NIV 2011)

Such modern prophecies should not be considered infallible. The prophets, however respected they may be as church leaders, are fallible human beings. Their utterances are not inspired Holy Scripture, not on the same level as the writings of the Old Testament prophetic authors—who were only a few of the many prophets operating in their time.

But when specific prophecies are made and come true, that tends to confirm the prophet and give greater credibility to his or her other prophecies. So it would be right for the people of the USA to take heed of Wilkerson's warnings for his home country: a massive earthquake following the one in Japan, and major rioting in New York and elsewhere.

These prophecies should be taken as conditional, if the nation does not repent, as was Jonah's biblical prophecy of the overthrow of one of the greatest cities of his world (Jonah 3:4). Also we don't know the time scales involved: if the Japan earthquake was nearly 40 years after the prophecy, the US one may be even further in the future. It is wise to be ready, but not to panic. Wilkerson's 2009 advice is good:

I will say to my soul: No need to run... no need to hide. This is God's righteous work. I will behold our Lord on his throne, with his eye of tender, loving kindness watching over every step I take—trusting that he will deliver his people even through floods, fires, calamities, tests, trials of all kinds.

We should also avoid giving these events too much significance. They do not mean that Jesus is about to come again. He clearly warned:

You will hear of wars and rumors of wars, but see to it that you are not alarmed. Such things must happen, but the end is still to come. Nation will rise against nation, and kingdom against kingdom. There will be famines and earthquakes in various places. All these are the beginning of birth pains.... Because of the increase of wickedness, the love of most will grow cold, but the one who stands firm to the end will be saved. And this gospel of the kingdom will be preached in the whole world as a testimony to all nations, and then the end will come.

—MATTHEW 24:6–8, 12–14 (NIV 2011)[1]

DAISY OSBORN'S END-TIME VISION

One of the co-authors was personal friends with Daisy Osborn; and even shopped at the same grocery store as T. L. and Daisy. His first recollection of the couple was at a local high school (Will Rogers High School) in Tulsa, Oklahoma, where T. L. Osborn and Daisy spoke, showing their beloved missions film, *Black Gold,* in 1956. A week before this writing, one co-author had dinner with the former General Manager for over 15 years of the T. L. Osborn Ministry Foundation, who also produced the *Black Gold* film. The following is an end-time vision experienced by Daisy Osborn.

> I lay sleepless and horrified, greatly vexed in the Spirit. The Lord visited and showed me things that will shortly come to pass. The *judgment* and *wrath* of God will soon bring disaster and havoc to the world we live in. The *die is cast.* God's clock is set. *Time* is running out.
>
> "In a *vision*" I saw: the face of the earth and the changing of the shape of America. It was drastically altered and reduced in size through terrible disasters. Hunger and suffering were everywhere. The devastation caused by volcanic eruptions and fires were widespread and horrifying during this terrible holocaust.
>
> I saw Christians clustering together from all walks of life and many church affiliations. They did not care about their sectarian doctrines. The tie that bound them in their desperate hour was their common faith

in Christ. They clung together as though their survival depended upon each other.

After these terrifying cataclysmic events which the Lord showed me, all the evils of sectarianism and apostasy vanished among the Christians desperate struggle to draw strength from one another. Those who had been lukewarm, cast aside besetting sins, and sought identity with the true believers. Cigarettes, pills, social drinkers, marital cheaters; were repented of and amends were made.

A new sense of values gripped the conscience of Believers. The new morality standard and modern license for laxity was like a remorseful hangover. Most of the Christians in the "visitation" were amazed that *we* "were experiencing" and *we* were witnessing His *wrath* and *judgment!*

Many social Christians were ill prepared. Their frivolous, unwatchful, imprudent lives had *gambled* on Mercy and Grace, which they had thought required no reckoning—*ever!*

I saw hordes (believers) lost among the religious and Christ Jesus rejecters. As I looked, I saw where mountains were flattened. Believers were *fleeing* to the desert to take shelter in caves and rocks. The *desolation* was so terrible that it seemed *no one* would be spared (Luke 21:34–36 (KJV) and Matthew 24:20–22).

All but a few were full of remorse. Lamentations could be heard everywhere. It was heartening to observe that during the *fearsome disasters—unshakable faith* held like an *anchor* among the Christians. They knew they would *soon* see the *Son* coming in the clouds of heaven and with Power and Glory!

[Daisy Osborn (now with the Lord) was the wife of Brother T.L. Osborn.][2]

DEMOS SHAKARIAN

One of the co-authors of this book was an International Director for FGBMFI for 25 years. In his book, *The Happiest People on Earth,* Demos Shakarian, founder of the Full Gospel Business Men's Fellowship International, tells about his father being prompted by the prophecy of a little boy, leading the entire family to move to the United States, where they escaped the near-annihilation of the Armenians through war.

> When he had finished, the manuscript was taken to people in the village who could read. It turned out that this illiterate child had written out in Russian characters a series of instructions and warnings. At some unspecified time in the future, the boy wrote, every Christian in Kara Kala would be in terrible danger. He foretold a time of unspeakable tragedy for the entire area, when hundreds of thousands of men, women, and children would be brutally murdered. The time would come, he warned, when everyone in the region must flee. They must go to a land across the sea. Although he had never seen a geography book, the Boy Prophet drew a map showing exactly where the fleeing Christians were to go. [To] the amazement of the adults, the body of water depicted so accurately in the drawing was not the nearby Black Sea, or the Caspian Sea, or even the farther-off Mediterranean, but the distant and unimaginable Atlantic Ocean! There was no doubt about it, nor about the identity of the land on the other side: the map plainly indicated the east coast of the United States of America.
>
> But the refugees were not to settle down there, the prophecy continued. They were to continue traveling

> until they reached the west coast of the new land. There, the boy wrote, God would bless them and prosper them, and cause their seed to be a blessing to the nations.
>
> A little later Efim also wrote out a second prophecy, but all anybody knew about that one was that it dealt with the still more distant future—when the people would once again have to flee [Authors' note: the West Coast in the future!]. Efim asked his parents to seal this prophecy in an envelope, and repeated the instructions he had received concerning it. He had been told in his vision that only a future prophet—chosen by the Lord for this task—could open the envelope and read the prophecy to the church. Anyone opening the envelope before this time would die.[3]

Efim, the little boy prophet from Armenia, helped to bring about the growth of the great organization, the Full Gospel Business Men's Fellowship International. His original prophecy to the Shakarian family caused the Shakarians to move to the United States, just in time to escape the Armenian massacre. His second prophecy dovetails with many other prophecies, which depict people having to literally flee the West Coast in the future, presumably by a flood caused by a devastating earthquake.

KEN PETERS: "I HAVE SEEN THE TRIBULATION"

Of course there are many voices out there, and some "prophetic" voices cannot be depended upon as genuinely being from God or the Holy Spirit. In these end-time days, Christians must be on guard and totally discerning.

> In 1980, Ken Peters had a long, detailed dream about the coming tribulation period. This article provides the transcript and video of his amazing testimony....
>
> Today, prophet Ken Peters and his wife Tonya are Senior Elders at the The Gathering @ Corona, which is an Apostolic Prophetic Reformation church.[4]

Here is a transcript of the prophecy via James Bailey of Z3 News (April 23, 2013). It is entitled: "I Have Seen the Tribulation":

> At the time I received this dream I was not even a believer in Jesus Christ. I was raised in the Catholic Church but had never personally invited the Lord Jesus to come into my heart to be my Lord. As a practicing Catholic, I had no knowledge of what the Bible said about the tribulation period or any of the events of the last days.

> When the dream began, I heard what sounded like a loud car horn. Then I saw people coming up out of their graves all over the world. People were not coming up out of every cemetery plot, just some of them. Even in the same cemetery there were other plots with nobody resurrected from them.
>
> These resurrections were very violent. It was like the earth was receiving a small explosion and breaking open. I literally saw dirt flying. This was happening all over the globe. Those who were resurrected were clothed in white robes. It looked like they were wearing choir robes. The light glimmered

off of their clothing. Their clothes and their bodies appear brighter than the sun. Their clothes made the men look very masculine and the women look very feminine. They looked mature but they did not look old. Those who had lost their hair had all of their hair back again. Young people who were resurrected were still young but yet had maturity about them.

All those who came out of the graves just disappeared. I never saw them go up into the clouds. They just vanished.

I did not see one single living person changed into a new body. I did not see any changes coming to any living person.

Mass Hysteria

As soon as the resurrected people disappeared from the earth mass hysteria spread across all the people left on the earth. People had the appearance of absolute despair. There was pandemonium everywhere. There was mass chaos, lawlessness, and fear everywhere. I was able to see in many quadrants of the earth and this was not just happening in one nation but it was all over the globe. The hysteria brought perplexity to just about everyone. Everyone had a look of hopelessness on their face. Nobody seemed to be happy about living. Lawlessness and fear permeated society completely.

No one was isolated from the despair that was hitting the world. No one was hidden from it. It was engulfing the whole globe. I was able to see into different regions and different continents and everyone was experiencing this. It was almost as though the whole world had become like a third world nation, completely behind the times.

It was like every person on earth had just left their mother's funeral. That's how people appeared. They were very grieving and despondent....

Earthquakes and Famines

While I was on my way to make a business transaction a very unusual thing happened. There was an earthquake while I was on my way to the bank. I was just entering the bank. Across the street from my bank there was a large seven-story building. This was a triangle looking building. It was all glass in its appearance. In this dream, an earthquake hit and began shaking this glass building. It fell over and killed about 200 people. This earthquake was massive. I know from what I saw with the globe shaking at this point that it was a worldwide earthquake.

The earthquake hit and there were multiple, millions of lives lost. The world was completely stunned. The devastation to property and loss of life was beyond comprehension. It could not be measured. Some regions were so destroyed that they never bothered to send rescue teams in. That's how devastated they were. This destruction was global. It reached the whole globe.

The earthquake caused a massive change in weather patterns. The normal weather patterns completely changed. The patterns for winter became summer and summer became winter. You might have a day of snow and a day of heat. The world was in total chaos in [these] weather patterns. Predicting the weather

> became totally impossible. It was just useless to try to forecast weather. Predictions did not work.
>
> Some very unusual things began to happen almost immediately. Crops began to perish due to droughts. I was able to see all over the [globe] the most fertile areas, the most fertile farming areas. I live at the time of this dream in the most fertile farming area in the whole world, the San Joaquin Valley of California. These areas were totally destroyed with drought and famine. Places that were once fertile were now arid deserts. It was almost hard to comprehend what I was seeing. It was almost immediate. It was like somebody just took things and twisted the whole order.
>
> The thing that was strange to me was that weather seemed to have its own mind. The earth being shaken from its axis manipulated the weather. I was above the earth and I saw it shaking. I saw the earth rocking around like it was a drunken person trying to walk. It was very frightening to me.
>
> I can't tell you how hopeless or empty I felt after seeing these things happening. Many times I wished I could have just woken up and pretended these things were not really happening.[5]

Our objective in this book is not to just show you "the way" about prophesied earthquakes, but to present to you a sampling of the many voices and respected prophets that are out there and displaying what they have to say about the future—*your* future!

Endnotes

1. See http://www.gentlewisdom.org/2575/davidwilkerson-prophecy-earthquakes-in-japan-and-usa.html.

2. See http://www.watchmanscry.com/forum/showthread.php?t=14272.

3. See http://www.endtimemanna.org/Magnusson/Data/Prophecy_of_the_Boy_Prophet.pdf.

4. See http://z3news.com/w/ken-peters-tribulation/.

5. Ibid.

Chapter 8

DUMITRU DUDUMAN TELLS OF A CALIFORNIA MEGA-QUAKE

DUMITRU DUDUMAN WAS a controversial, yet truthful, modern-day prophet. He passed away in 1997. Before we study his prophecies, it is important to understand Dumitru's background and what he came out of.

Dumitru and his wife Maria were from Northern Romania and lived on a small farm close to the Soviet border. He pastored a small country church near their farm. Over an 18-year period, he secretly delivered hundreds of thousands of Bibles and aid to the Soviet Union.

In 1980, Dumitru delivered over 100,000 New Testaments which were used extensively at the Moscow Olympics. In August of 1980, Dumitru was arrested, imprisoned, and interrogated for five months. He was beaten almost every day and repeatedly shocked in an electric chair. Arrest and interrogation became a continuous way of life for Dumitru. In 1983 he was hung by his waist and beaten on three different occasions. He suffered nine broken ribs and deformities on his rib cage.

Finally, the authorities gave Dumitru three choices: a mental hospital, prison, or expulsion to the United States. The choice was hard for Dumitru because of his loyalty to his homeland, but he felt his first loyalty was to God. They packed their clothes and most prized possessions, but the officials refused to let them take anything, so they left their homeland and friends empty-handed. God gave Dumitru a powerful message for America. The message was hard, and many people were unable to receive it, but the Lord promised victory to those who listened.[1]

Dumitru Duduman was born to George and Escaterina Duduman on July 14, 1932, in Hintesti, Romania. His native village is situated in the northeastern part of Romania near the Russian border. Here Dumitru was brought up in the knowledge of God by his parents, but most of all from his grandfather, Costache, whom he loved deeply. He grew accustomed to religious persecution at a very young age seeing his father and older brother, Costache, put in prison for their beliefs. Although the rest of the family had not been arrested, they were ordered to hard labor in the Communist farmland projects....

It was also during this time that persecution against Christians began to escalate. Dumitru was given orders to search every ship coming into the Constanta harbor at the Black Sea. If he should find Bibles, he was to confiscate them and arrest whomever was responsible for bringing them into the country.

One morning as he and eight of his men were searching a ship, Dumitru came upon a large number of Bibles. He was overjoyed at finding the Bibles knowing that this would bring yet another upgrade in his ranking.

While questioning the man who was responsible for bringing the Bibles, Dumitru had his first personal encounter with the power of God. He heard a

> voice telling him to help the man unload the Bibles and cause him no harm. When the voice persisted, Dumitru obeyed and helped the missionary to the fullest....
>
> In 1973 Dumitru began smuggling large quantities of Bibles over the Russian border. He had established many connections with outside missionaries who would supply him with Bibles. Through many miraculous [occurrences], God continually protected Dumitru. In one instance, God even blinded the eyes of the police so they would not see the car filled with Bibles that he was riding in. In all of his years of smuggling Bibles he was never caught. In 1979 based on information received from informants within the Christian church, Dumitru was arrested and brutally tortured for over five months.... While Dumitru was in prison, God spoke to him through an angel, encouraging him not to fear for he still had much work to do.... Over a fifteen-year period, with God's help, Dumitru smuggled more than 300,000 Bibles and New Testaments into Russia alone, not taking into account the number of Bibles that he distributed throughout Romania.[2]

Dumitru graduated to heaven in May of 1997. Michael Boldea, Jr., the grandson of Prophet Dumitru Duduman, continues the prophetic tradition by making statements about the California mega-quake that is to come. He communicated the following on February 3, 2006:

A Great Earthquake Coming

> Isaiah 24:19–20, "The earth is violently broken, the earth is split open, the earth is shaken exceedingly.

The earth shall reel to and fro like a drunkard, and shall totter like a hut; its transgression shall be heavy upon it, and it will fall, and not rise again."

While I was in Romania, one night after my devotions I went to bed, exhausted and in need of much sleep having ridden in a truck all day delivering food to families. It had been a hard day, and we had to push the truck out of snow banks and ditches more than once. My body ached, and all I really wanted was to get some good rest.

As I fell into a deep sleep I had a dream. I dreamt I was in a hotel room, asleep, when the bed began to shake violently. I knew what was happening right away. Having lived in California in the 1980s I was keenly aware of what an earthquake felt like. Suddenly I was no longer in bed, but high above San Francisco Bay, looking down on the Golden Gate Bridge. As I watched it, it began to shudder, break apart, and fall into the waters below. I continued to watch the devastation, seeing buildings collapse, and masses of people trying to find shelter. Then a voice spoke out of the heavens, a voice I had never heard before, a voice of great authority. "I will shake this land from its foundations, such as the eyes of this generation has not seen. The world will stand in awe, and tremble in fear, as even the very geography of this nation will be transformed. My wrath is ready to be poured out, for sin has overrun My temple."

In my dream I began to weep, not due to the devastation I was seeing, but due to the great power of the voice I was hearing. I woke up trembling, unable to breathe, and tired as I was I could not go to sleep again.

Shortly before sunrise, my phone began to ring, and when I answered it, it was my brother Daniel. "Are you awake?" he asked. "Yes," I answered.

"I had a dream last night," he continued, "It was a terrible dream. I dreamt of a big earthquake coming to America."

When I told him I'd had the same dream, he was silent for some time, then said, "I'm coming over so we [can] pray."

He had just arrived at my apartment, when my phone rang again. It was a brother from 200 kilometers away, who is prophetically gifted, and has spoken many words over me that have come to pass.

"Is this Mike?" When I answered in the affirmative, he said, "I had a dream last night, and I felt I needed to call and tell you about it. I dreamt of a terrible earthquake in your country. I saw a big bridge that just collapsed. I saw destruction as I have never seen before. Does this mean anything to you?"

It took me some time to find something to say. I was speechless, and could find no words. On the same night, three different people had the same dream, with the same vivid details. Knowing that the brother had a prayer group that met nightly, I asked him to remember America in their prayers whenever they prayed, and he said he would. Before he hung up he said, "Mike, I've had many dreams in my life, the Lord willed it so, but none has scared me as the dream I had last night. Only God can protect someone through something like that; there is no other hope but to run to Him."

No matter what may come upon this land, we know that God abides with His faithful, keeping them, guiding them, and protecting them. Events will begin

> to unfold upon this earth, that will make even the mightiest of men tremble in fear, but knowing that we have a shelter from the storm, a sovereign God who watches over us, fearlessly we press on faithful in all that He asks of us.
>
> Psalm 91:7–11, "A thousand may fall at your side, and ten thousand at your right hand; but it shall not come near you. Only with your eyes shall you look, and see the reward of the wicked. Because you have made the Lord, who is my refuge, even the Most High, your habitation, no evil shall befall you, nor shall any plague come near your dwelling; for He shall give His angels charge over you, to keep you in all your ways."[3]

Dumitru Duduman, like many other prophets, has predicted that a mega-quake will hit California. It is quite heartening to see the mantle of prophecy moving from one generation to the next.

Furthermore, to have three of Dumitru's sons receive the same prophetic dream at the exact time in three different places is a genuine miracle. As terrifying as it is that all three dreamed about the collapse of the San Francisco Golden Gate Bridge due to an earthquake, they each commented upon this tragedy and presented a true and genuine hope for God's faithful. They described it as a "shelter in the time of storm" to those who are faithful to our Lord! Is that you?

ENDNOTES

1. See http://www.ubm1.org/?page=dumitru.
2. See https://www.handofhelp.com/about_dumitru.php.
3. See http://www.ubml1.org/scmegaquake.html.

Chapter 9

REV. JAMES BAKKER TELLS OF HIS CALIFORNIA EARTHQUAKE VISION

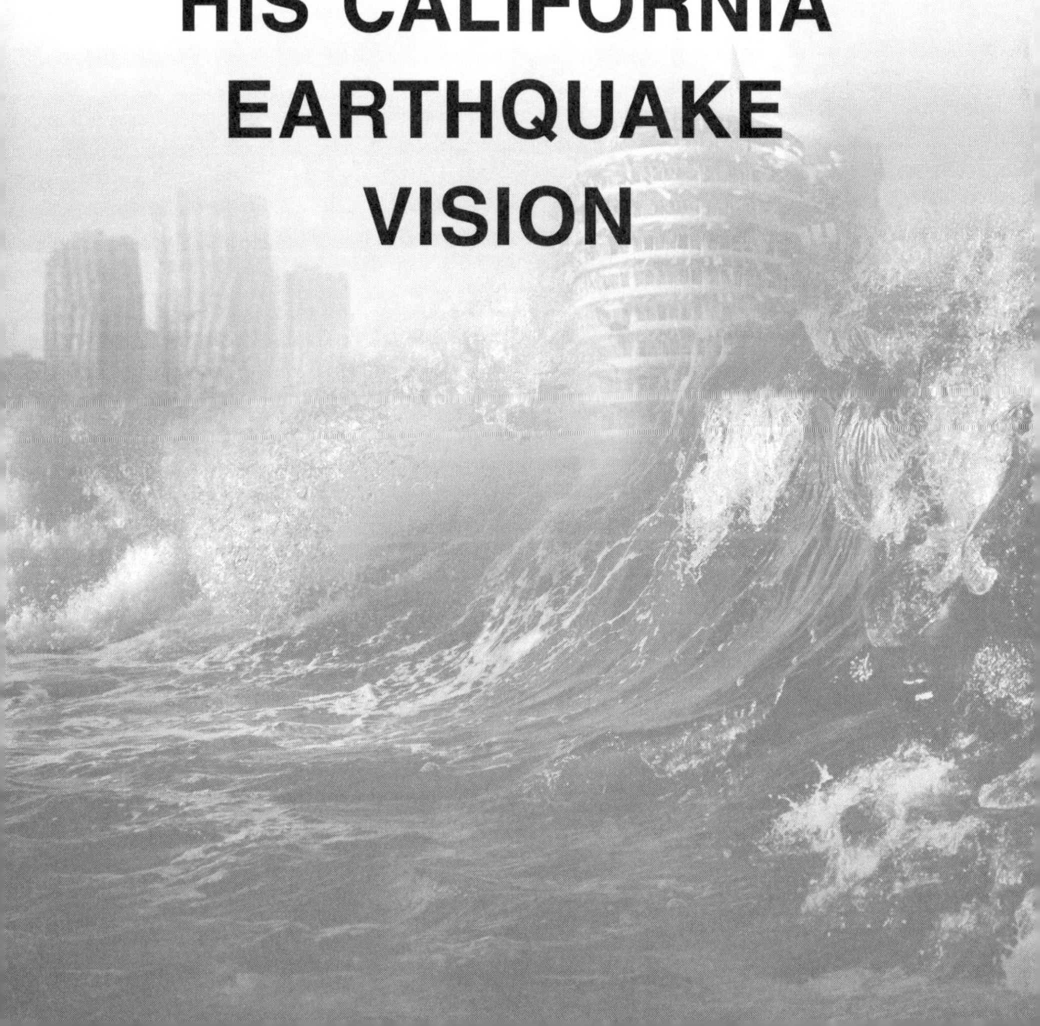

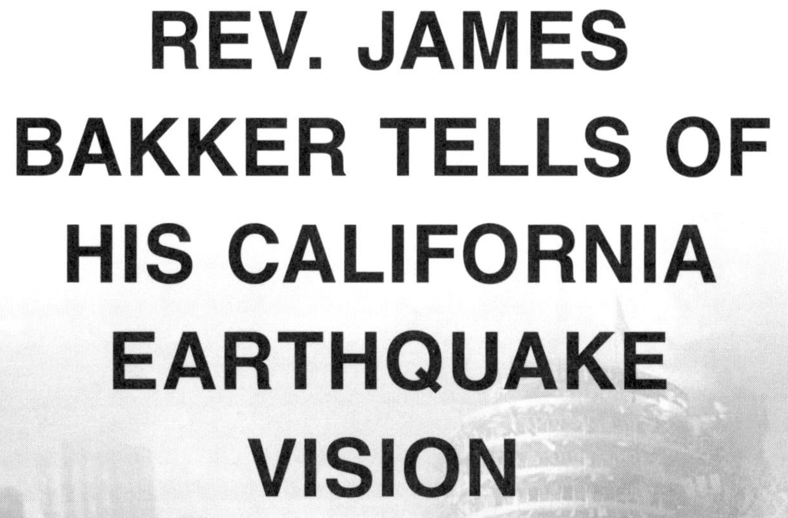

REV. JIM BAKKER really does not need any introduction. Years ago, he was a household word as he founded and hosted the PTL Club television broadcast for many years.

Jim is once again "back in the saddle" as host of his own daily television program, much of it dedicated to the end-times and the various prophecies that surround those big events. In fact, Rev. Jim Bakker is utilizing the media to warn people of the dramatic events of the end-time, which includes earthquakes. Since he is on the literal frontlines of informing the greatest number of people, via his television programs, of end-times events, it is only appropriate to share some of the "earthquake insights" that he provides in his great book, *Prosperity and the Coming Apocalypse,* which he co-wrote with Ken Abraham.

> At the risk of sounding like an alarmist, I feel compelled to report an unusual personal experience that causes me to believe a major earthquake will soon shake Los Angeles to its foundations. In 1997, I traveled to L.A. to appear on the CNN broadcast of Larry King Live and to speak at several churches in California. I arrived at night, and a chauffeured limousine picked me up. I was thankful for the ride, but a little uneasy about getting into the limo. In the years since I lost PTL, I had become much more comfortable riding in my Jeep.

Nevertheless, the *Larry King Show* had provided the transportation, so I gratefully climbed into the back seat of the stretch limo and settled in for the ride to my hotel. As we drove from the airport toward the bright lights in the heart of L.A., I experienced one of the strangest sensations of my life. It was as though my body became a human Geiger counter; I started resonating with the earth deep below Los Angeles. I began to shake and suddenly, in the Spirit, it was as if I could see down into the earth. I saw huge boulders, bowed upward and grinding against each other, like one fist pushing against another.

The Lord began to speak to my heart and mind as clearly as if He had called me on the limo's car phone. "This is the pressure of the ages," the Lord revealed to me. "And it's about to let go." Trembling, I looked out the car window, just as the limo whisked past the beautiful, statuesque skyscrapers in downtown L.A. It was then that I sensed God speaking to me, words I am reluctant to actually put in print, yet words that have been seared for all eternity into my spirit.

As I stared at the tall buildings, the Lord said to me, "Not one of these buildings will be left standing. There is going to be an earthquake unlike any other earthquake this area has experienced. There will be nothing left."

I shuddered in shock, shaking as if trying to awaken from a bad dream. But this was no dream and I was fully awake. As we drove further away from downtown, the sensation subsided, and the Geiger-counter effect stopped. Looking back, I believe God was impressing upon me once again that I must proclaim this message before it is too late.

> Despite the increase in natural disasters, Jesus cautioned us about becoming overly agitated about these things. He said, "But all these things are merely the beginning of birth pangs" (Matthew 24:8 NASB). As any mother knows, the closer the labor pains get, the shorter the interval of time between contractions, the closer it is to the birth of the baby. Jesus was saying that we should regard the prevalence of earthquakes, famines, and other natural disasters similarly. These are warning signs, alerting us that something significant is going to happen soon.[1]

Rev. James Bakker has an enormous following of many millions of people. The words he has heard from the Lord about the future are very bold. One may be tempted to dismiss this shocking prophetic vision of the Los Angeles skyline disappearing. According to Rev. Bakker, "There will be nothing left."

However, when one continues to view his television broadcasts and observes the numerous well-known prophets who frequent his show, there is an urgent sense that one can feel "in the Spirit" that these cataclysmic events will truly happen. Millions have become believers in these prophecies due to Bakker's persuasive and informed research about earthquakes.

Endnote

1. Jim Bakker and Ken Abraham, *Prosperity and the Coming Apocalypse* (Nashville, TN: Thomas Nelson Publishers, 1998), 110–111.

Chapter 10

PROPHET BOB JONES PROPHESIES THE FUTURE

Bob Jones was a contemporary prophet with a tremendous love for the Lord Jesus and His truth. His prophecies have spanned over three decades as the Lord enabled him to foretell earthquakes, tidal waves, comets, and weather patterns. Bob often told leaders their dreams and experiences, as well as the interpretations. Over the past three decades, Bob Jones moved with a clear revelatory gifting, accompanied by gifts of healings and miracles.

After overseeing a prophetic ministry for over four decades, Bob Jones "graduated to heaven" on February 14, 2014. His prophecies were on the forefront about what the future holds, especially when it comes to earthquakes.

On New Year's Eve, 1997, before most of the prophecies were given about earthquakes, there was a New Year's Eve Prophetic Conference held at Rick Joyner's Morning Star Ministries in Charlotte, North Carolina. The conference speakers were Bob Jones, Jim Bakker, and Rick Joyner. Here are excerpts from that historic conference:

> I [God] have been showing My prophets these things for years. Now walk into it. I am beginning to perform My word.
>
> Bob Jones saw two mighty angels. One was holding the "San Diego plate" and the other, the New Madrid Fault Line. When each cup is full the angel will turn loose and the quakes will happen. They will be *sudden*.

VISION OF CALIFORNIA EARTHQUAKE(S)

Mammoth Lake [east of Modesto, California] is "going to happen" with an enormous earthquake and / or volcanic eruption.

When Mammoth Lake quakes / erupts, Hoover Dam will burst. Water flumes, including those to Southern California, will break apart. 25,000,000 people in the Southwest will be affected and without water. *Lack of water will be the main danger in California.*

Death Valley will become a great Inland Sea.

In the California quake Bob saw the ground quake for *five* minutes. The ground liquefied, and complete houses and buildings sank into the ground just as if they were in quicksand.

The San Fernando Valley—seat of pornography—won't rise again.

Los Angeles: *get out!* Expect a devastating earthquake and terrorist attack(s) with nuclear suitcase bombs. Some of these bombs have already been smuggled into California. 126 nuclear suit case bombs are missing from the USSR. Many have been smuggled into the USA and Israel by terrorists.

Due to the eruptions / earthquake a plate will separate. The Sea of Cortez (Gulf of California) to the Los Angeles River will separate from the continental USA. What is left of Baja California and Southern California east of the breaking / sliding continental plate will be an island or series of islands.

The cup is nearly full for California. [12-31-97] Expect quakes, terrorist bombs and viruses. Get into your prayer closet!

Vision of a New Madrid Earthquake

There will be an enormous earthquake somewhere along the New Madrid fault line. A mighty angel has been holding this fault line together also.

Six great cities will be destroyed. Among them are Chicago, Morgan City, St. Louis, and Memphis. Memphis will become a lake. The Mississippi River will be 35 miles wide when it is all over. The shaking will be felt all the way to Charlotte, North Carolina. Water from the Great Lakes will flow south into the Mississippi River and then into the Gulf of Mexico.

Other General Prophetic Words

Our economy will be destroyed when a huge earthquake hits Tokyo and the Japanese pull their money out of the U.S. stock market. [Author's note: Prophetess Catherine Browne of Scotland had a vision some years ago of a horrific eruption of Mt. Fuji, which caused massive destruction in Tokyo and worldwide mourning.]

This nation will repent when our cities are leveled.

Some Midwest cities are going to experience 5 feet of rain in 2–3 days.

There will be a Third World War

There will be signs in the sun and the earth will change. See Gen. 10:25.

These are very sober times, but be of good cheer. Get your eyes off the gifts and onto the giver of the gifts, the Creator. Get to know the Lord as a wife knows her husband. If there is trouble in your marriage, fix it! Put on Christ![1]

Speaking at a "Blue Moon Conference," Bob Jones shared the following prophetic word regarding a coming earthquake in California.

"I believe the next one is getting ready to happen when this volcano will erupt when the plates can't take the pressure anymore. And I believe the pressure are melting the plates down there to where this has got to be vented, and these earthquakes are just a sign of what is getting ready to happen. It's getting ready to blow! When it does, it will break loose all the way to the Sea of Cortez, right up the Los Angeles River. And that plate in there will separate from the United States, and you can drive a boat up that river. You can go from the Gulf of Cortez to the Pacific Ocean. And Death Valley will be a great inland sea. And we aren't far from that."

There is no date given regarding this earthquake. However, Bob Jones has been warning about it since the 1980s. The Lord told him there would be two signs that would mark the season when the earthquake is getting close. The first sign is a major earthquake would hit Japan. The second sign is large numbers of dead fish would wash up on the shore on the California coast. Both of these events happened in 2011. So now that those events have happened, the earthquake could hit at any time.

This same word has also been received by other highly respected men of God, including Rick Joyner of Morning Star Ministries. Rick Joyner also received this word many years ago. For years people who were living in California would ask him if they should move away. He told them to stay there

> unless the Lord told them to leave. However, after the signs of its coming were fulfilled, Rick Joyner sought the Lord about what to tell the people who came to him seeking direction. He said the Lord told him to tell them, "Don't stay unless you hear the Lord tell you to stay."[2]

Rick Joyner, a well-known prophet in the United States, did dedicate the "Bob Jones Memorial Center," with a plaque which reads:

> Our spiritual father and dear friend to the ministry, Bob Jones, went home to be with the Lord on February 14, 2014. MorningStar is honoring his life by restoring the historical "Tram Stop" located right across from the main entrance to Heritage and calling it the Bob Jones Memorial Center. Bob Jones walked past this building almost daily during his times of prayer and talking to his Papa. This multipurpose facility will serve to carry forward Bob's vision of seeing the one billion soul harvest released on the earth today.
>
> In 1975, the Lord told Bob Jones, "Prepare the people, for I am going to bring a billion souls in one great harvest, and most of them are going to be youth." In 1983, thirty-one years before his death, he had another encounter where he saw his tombstone. From his death a beautiful rose of Sharon would spring forth, symbolizing the body of Christ united in the first commandment. In 2014, the Lord spoke to Bob and Bonnie Jones that prayer, praise, and prophecy would be instrumental in the fulfillment of Bob's lasting vision.

> The Bob Jones Memorial Center will carry his vision forward with daily prayer, worship, and other relevant events. This building was a central meeting place during PTL days and will be a strategic hub for the ingathering at MorningStar… The restored building will serve as a memorial stone, or an "Ebenezer," to commemorate Bob's life and work. This will also be a reminder of what MorningStar has been called to do here on this property.[3]

For almost half a century, Prophet Bob Jones has been prophesying about the end of the age. Many of his prophecies have been "right on"; therefore, he has many followers. His prophecy regarding the drought in California (including 25 million people without water), for instance, is nearly coming to pass, as of the writing of this book. Many, however, question his prophecy with relation to the bursting of the Hoover Dam due to earthquakes.

Remember, "test the spirits" by praying to our Heavenly Father for divine direction for your individual life, especially with regard to acting upon prophecies.

ENDNOTES

1. See http://www.standeyo.com/NEWS/11_Prophecy/110317.Bob.Jones.EQ.html.
2. See http://z3news.com/w/bob-jones-prophecy-earthquake-hit-california/.
3. 3. See http://www.morningstarministries.org/bob-jones-memorial-center.

Chapter 11

RICK JOYNER GIVES AN END-TIME WARNING

RICK JOYNER IS probably the best-known, modern-day prophet alive today. Therefore, we are compelled to display a couple of his main prophecies, in conjunction with those of Bob Jones, that deal with earthquakes.

> Rick Joyner is Founder and Executive Director of MorningStar Ministries and Heritage International Ministries. Rick is President of The Oak Initiative, an interdenominational movement that mobilizes Christians to engage in the great issues of our time. He has authored more than forty books, including The Final Quest Trilogy, There Were Two Trees in the Garden, and A New America. Rick and his wife, Julie, have five children: Anna Jane, Aaryn, Amber, Ben, and Sam.[1]

> In the mid-1990s Joyner, already president of MorningStar publications, located at that time in Charlotte, North Carolina, worked with Reggie White, who was planning to purchase Jim Bakker's defunct resort, Heritage USA. In 1999 White, having failed to purchase the property, continued to work with Joyner on plans to build a biblical theme park.
>
> In 2004 MorningStar purchased part of the Heritage USA complex (originally established by Bakker and PTL in Fort Mill, South Carolina) for $1.6

million. The complex has been renamed Heritage International Ministries.[2]

In his 2011 "Special Bulletin #1," entitled "The Day the World Changed," Rick Joyner wrote,

> There are demarcation points in history where a turn is made and the world starts down a different path. March 11, 2011 will be remembered as one of those days. The 9.0 earthquake that rocked Japan, moving the entire island an estimated 8 feet, actually shifted the earth on its axis enough to change the length of our days and nights. It may not have been enough to notice, but even a slight change on our axis can have major consequences over time. The same is true with the social and economic consequence this earthquake, tsunami, and nuclear meltdown will have on modern civilization.
>
> It was twenty-two years ago that I first heard Bob Jones talk about a major earthquake that would be coming to Japan. He said that it would set off cataclysmic events. Thousands have heard Bob predict quakes and other natural events with astonishing accuracy. One of the most dramatic was the last San Francisco quake. He foresaw that the quake would be centered in Northern California but south of San Francisco. He said that it would be 7.0 on the Richter scale, that the bridges would be dangerous, and that "the world will witness it." Bob shared this at conferences and churches for months before it hit that fall. It struck during the first game of the World Series that year, which was being played in San Francisco, and it was being broadcast to 160 nations who witnessed it

live, accurately fulfilling all that Bob had predicted, including how the world would see it.

Many prophetic people were shown the next quake that hit Southern California, and they were told that this was a warning of another much greater one to come. We shared this in many churches and conferences in Southern California. When it struck, we were astonished at how even the churches responded, downplaying its message, and some even boasting that Californians could handle anything. We felt that the quake we had clearly predicted, with many details that were accurate, had virtually no impact on the people, even some of the strongest Christians who had heard the warnings.

When one of the most well-known Christian leaders in the area asked me what could be done to delay or lessen this quake, I was given "a word of wisdom" that the only commandment with a promise was to honor our fathers and mothers, and the promise was that *"it may be well with you, and that you may live long on the earth" (see Ephesians 6:3).* The Lord showed me that one way we could do this was the way Israel did it, which was to drink from the wells that our fathers have dug. Spiritually, this meant to partake of their teachings. When I preached this in Pasadena, Lou Engle picked it up, wrote a book about it, and has in a most remarkable way carried this message to the nation through The Call.

Has it worked? I think Lou's work and that of many others have given us the time that we've had. While many were still receiving revelation about the coming big one, and many were expecting it, Bob Jones was adamant that it would not come until the major one hit Japan that he had seen. When the major quake hit Kobe, Japan, Bob was sure that was not the one he had seen. When Bob walked into the service last Sunday after the recent 9.0 quake, tsunami, and nuclear meltdown, I immediately asked him if this was the one. I've never seen such concern in Bob's face as he answered, "You know what this means."

WHAT DOES IT MEAN?

It marks a demarcation point after which great change will come to the whole world, including an ultimate meltdown of the economy. It will also be followed by a major quake on the West Coast of the United States.

Of course, when and where on the west coast that this major quake is going to hit are important questions. Bob was not given a timing of this quake but was only told that it would not come before the big one he had been shown in Japan. Now it can come. However, this does not necessarily mean that it is immediate. It could come today, or it could still be years away. We are praying that it still will be delayed so that everyone who will hear the warning, and should move, will be able to do this in an orderly way.

This does not mean that everyone there, even those who may be near ground zero, should move. Some may be called by God to stay and be used during this impending catastrophe. However, until now, we have counseled all who asked if they should leave the West Coast not to do this unless they heard from the Lord to do so. Now we will begin counseling everyone to leave unless they hear from the Lord to stay.

Until now, I have prayed for leaders who would have the understanding, wisdom, and courage to make the changes needed to avoid this economic meltdown.

> Now I am praying for leaders with the understanding, wisdom, and courage to lead us through what is now inevitable.

The Nature of Prophecy

> As we are told in I Corinthians 13, we see in part, know in part, and prophesy in part. No one has the whole picture, so to get the whole picture, we need to put the parts together. This is why in the Scriptures that say such things as in Amos 3:7, *"Surely the Lord GOD does nothing unless He reveals His secret counsel to His servants the prophets,"* it is always plural, not just a single prophet. No one prophet, or prophetic movement, has the whole revelation. That is a major reason why we need each other.[3]

Rick Joyner has been a catalyst for many known prophets. He states regarding his prophetic leadership:

> We know many prophetically gifted people who have seen different aspects of this major quake coming. I do not know anyone at this writing who has what I consider to be a trustworthy timing on it. We will seek to compile these prophecies and share anything we feel is important in future Special Bulletins. As we are told in Proverbs 4:18, *"the path of the righteous is like the light of dawn, that shines brighter and brighter until the full day."* It is as we walk and as we need it that the Lord tends to give us more insight. I am just sharing what we do have now.[4]

James Bailey of Z3 News writes,

In February, 2013, a panel of prophetic ministers met at the Morningstar Advanced Prophetic Ministry Conference. They shared what Lord has shown them regarding a major earthquake coming on the west coast of the United States from San Diego, California to Seattle, Washington.

The ministers included Rick Joyner, Bob Jones, and Paul Keith Davis. Rick Joyner and Bob Jones first saw these events back in the 1970s and 1980s. They are raising the topic now because they believe the time for the earthquake is coming soon because the events that they were shown that would precede the west coast quake have now happened, including the Japanese earthquake that hit there in 2011. They are warning people to move away from the west coast unless God specifically tells them to stay there.

The partial transcript of their comments is provided here:

Bob Jones: Off of San Diego, dolphins have come together from I don't know how many places they would have to come together but they are seven miles long and five miles wide swimming from San Diego. I really feel that this is a warning. Nature is warning us.

Rick Joyner and I wrote warnings on this in 1989. Why would that many dolphins come together? Dolphins are on top of the water. I wonder what is going on under the water. [Nature] hears its warnings before things happen. We ought to be praying for the United States because I think things are getting ready to happen from San Diego to Seattle. That is what the Lord told me a few years ago. Why would they be leaving?

Rick Joyner and I were not together at the same time in California in 1989. We both got prophecies, we saw things of a coming earthquake that is beyond anything you can imagine. I have known that there is an Archangel holding the place together in California. Has California grieved the Father so much that He has taken his hand off of California? Then we need to begin to pray for California to where there will be that mercy and that grace.

Rick Joyner: One of the things the Lord showed us, He showed us the big one that is coming, but He showed us a warning quake too. We went around and we had specific details, and it all happened and it was shocking to us. One of the biggest shocks was how, even though we had specifics, and it was clear, and it happened just like we said, many of the church leaders said, "We don't believe that." It was about as clear of a warning shot as it could be and yet they said no, that is just nature. That was the shocking part to me.

We really need to pray for hearing ears. There really is a spirit of delusion as I talked about yesterday and as the apostle Paul warned there would be those who would only want their ears tickled, who could not hear these things.

We really need to pray for California. We need to pray for the whole West Coast, but there are some who hear. The encouraging thing lately is that some who had been the most adamant and saying, "This is not God. We don't believe this." They have had their own dreams and their own visions and their own revelation and now they really understand and know that this is really coming down. This (earthquake) is really happening.

I continue to pray for more time to get more people ready. But regardless of what happens in the natural, through human conflict or whatever, we have to get used to it being harvest time. We have to understand we are not going to run from this. We are going to run to it. It says in Joshua when they crossed over the Jordan River, the Jordan River overflowed all of its banks all of the days of the harvest. The Jordan River speaks of death. That is why Jesus baptized there and John baptized there. It empties into the Dead Sea.

We really are coming into Psalm 91 when 1,000 may fall at our side and 10,000 over here. We have to stay focused and do our job. Death has been swallowed up in victory. It is something we are not afraid of. It happens. We have to learn to stay focused and keep doing our job, but we have to learn also to run to those situations, not away from them.

We have been saying for years now, "Unless you hear God say to stay, get out." I felt like one of the things the Lord showed us that would precede this was the Japanese quake and tsunami. I felt years ago the Lord said that when that happened tell everyone to move away from those areas who have not heard to stay. We put that warning out. We keep it out. I get asked all the time, "Well it hasn't happened yet. It must not have been the Lord."

Listen, there are prophecies in Scriptures that took hundreds of years to happen. We have had many that took 20 years to happen. I don't know when it is going to happen. I believe the Lord is going to give us something specific. I feel very much that it is imminent. The last several days I have had this foreboding, a spiritual foreboding. Everything in the natural is going better than ever. In the natural I don't have any reason to feel this way. Something is going on. When I read about those dolphins I said, "This is not good."

It is proven that dolphins sense earthquakes days ahead of time. There is something that happens regarding the magnetics of the area, but as far as anyone knows what is going on right now with those dolphins out there is unprecedented. Nobody has heard anything quite like it.

I am praying for California and I am praying for such a revival and praying, "Lord, lessen this if there is any way that it can be spared because of revival and turning to the Lord." Who knows what He might do. We really need to be praying for our West Coast. The Lord is deeply offended by the poison, the spiritual and moral poison that is coming out of Hollywood. This is a terrible grief and He is not going to put up with it for much longer.

Bob Jones: Years ago, I don't remember how long, but I think it was in the mid-70s, the Lord told me that he is going to give them a warning in California. The shaking will begin in Caliente and Mexicali. When those two places shake, it will shortly happen in the other places. So I think if people will listen, He is going to warn them. I think the warning will be Mexicali and Caliente on the borderline. I think it is shortly going to shake. If it does, then San Diego, Los Angeles, San Francisco, and right up the coast. I have never known which was going to go first, San Francisco or Los Angeles. But I have seen the tsunami that will come [to] the Los Angeles River. The height of it is beyond imagination. In places it looked to me like it was over 200 feet tall.

Now what is your part? Your part is to get it into your soul that these things are going to come and you are going to go through them. They are not going to take you under. You are going to go through them. Every bad thing that has happened in your lifetime, you are here and it is a sign that you went through them. You survived them. This is what I think the Holy Spirit has been doing in your lives is bringing you to a place of faith to where you can survive what takes place when the Father removes his hand. And the Father is removing His hand off of certain areas right now. I believe this area that I am in here (near Fort Mill, South Carolina) is an area of safety. I was told to come here. The first place I was told was to go to Statesville, NC. Then I was told to move from Statesville to where I am right now. I have had him to tell me to move from certain areas at different times. I think for many of you, find out what area He wants you in, for there are going to be cities of refuge that are not even touched. There are going to be some states that are hardly touched. There are going to be other states that are demolished.

I brought a word about 11 northeast states, that the Father was removing His hand from them. It was about six months ago. I shared why the Father was removing his hand from them. It was because they all agreed on the same-sex marriage. So the Father, as to whether He is judging them one way or not, when He removes his hand, what do you think is going to happen? Judgment. So for those 11 northeast states, just look at what has happened to them. You take Christ out of the schools and you have dead babies. You take Christ out of the marketplace and you have an economy falling. You take Him out of the protection on the lines and you have dead cities. Those hurricanes, those bridges falling, that death, if that young man that did all the killing (in Connecticut) had been introduced to Christ in school that killing would have never happened. One of our jobs of the last days is going to be bringing Christ back into the schools.

I don't know how long some of the states are going to take their punishment because they don't have a covering. I would be terrified if I did not have Christ in my heart. You're talking about eternity in hell eternally. I wish that I had the ability to show the people on the earth what hell is like. The Lord has taken me there a couple of times. I don't want to ever go there again. But hell is real and so is heaven. You are on your way to heaven, but a lot of these jokers and everything are on their way to hell. They don't know what they are on their way to.

With what the Father breathed into Adam all men become eternal. God put His conscience inside of them. So when you are conceived, a part of God the Father comes into you and becomes your conscience.... This life down here is just like a drop in the bucket. It is so quick, but it determines where you will spend eternity.

I have seen heaven more than twice, and it is so beautiful. Everything there is beauty. Everything there is light. There are praises continually there. The mountains and everything up there are beautiful. The colors are beyond imagination to spend eternity there with Christ and with your brothers and sisters.[5]

Certainly, Rick Joyner is the most visible and prolific prophet today; his prophetic newsletter is one of the most-read publications. Though his writings point out earthquake devastation, they are reasonable and accessible to most level-headed, thinking people. He is not selfish, like many other prophets, because he shares prophecies from others. In fact, he helps to promote other prophets, especially when their prophecies come to pass. His reasonable approach is reaffirmed when he writes about an impending earthquake in California: "Do not leave California unless you hear from God."

In Rick Joyner's writings, the earthquake warnings go far beyond natural disasters. He warns that earthquakes will also mean economic disaster to some nations. The important thing that Rick emphasizes is that this period before earthquake devastation gives time for an enormous spiritual harvest time for the kingdom of God!

ENDNOTES

1. See http://www.morningstarministries.org/biographies/rick-joyner#.Vc40onFVhBc.
2. See https://en.wikipedia.org/wiki/Rick_Joyner.
3. See http://www.morningstarministries.org/resources/special-bulletins/2011/day-world-changed#.Vc41NXFVhBc.
4. Ibid.
5. See http://z3news.com/w/prophetic-warning-major-west-coast-earthquake-coming/.

Chapter 12

CATACLYSMIC WORLDWIDE EARTHQUAKE

WE DO NOT necessarily believe in a cataclysmic ending of the world before the "rapture" of the saints. However, we need to present an earthquake point of view that is held by numerous end-time prophets, and their followers, today.

Many believe in earthquakes happening in *every* place, not just in diverse places. Of course this results in devastating consequences upon the entire human race. Even the mention of the ramifications of these beliefs causes chills to run up and down everyone's spine.

One of the outstanding scholarly voices of this movement is Tim McHyde.

> Since 1999, Tim McHyde has researched and answered over 40,000 questions on Bible prophecy from visitors to his website, *EscapeAllTheseThings.com*. By adhering to Jesus' literal interpretation approach (John 10:35), Tim has been able to make sense of the hard passages that other teachers neglect, like "Wormwood" (Rev. 8:11). Tim's book *Know the Future* lays out the entire end time roadmap ahead for believers today, bringing comfort to readers previously scared or confused by Bible prophecy.[1]

One of the articles found on McHyde's website lays out his end-time thoughts:

JESUS TOLD HIS DISCIPLES ONE SIGN OF THE END, BUT DO YOU UNDERSTAND IT?

Jesus' disciples asked Jesus the very question that every Christian still wonders today: how do we know when you're coming back? Amazingly, Jesus answered by giving the actual "signs of his coming and the end of the age." He didn't refuse! We can read his straightforward answer in Matthew, Mark and Luke. Yet Christians don't understand his answer as evidenced by how they fall for every speculative counterfeit end time sign theory hatched by prophecy writers in its place. Find out what you've been missing in Jesus' answer so you understand the real signs of his coming and never have to fall for another false prophecy theory again.

JESUS' ANSWER TO THE BIGGEST QUESTION CHRISTIANS HAVE

When asked by the disciples, "Tell us...what is the sign of your coming and of the end of the age?" (Mt 24:3) Jesus did not refuse to answer. He plainly told them what to look for in the future to know when he was coming and when he was not. His answer began with two preliminary signs that would happen long before the end and ended with a few of the actual signs of the end and his coming just like the disciples requested. This made for a very balanced and clear answer. Or so you would think.

You've probably read Jesus' answer on these end time signs dozens of times. But I guarantee you have never understood it because there is a major problem with it.

Nevertheless, you may think you do. I've met many who claim to.

However, if you did understand the answer, you would have confidence to make long term plans like marrying or remarrying, having a child or another child, moving or buying a home or going back to school for further education, starting a business, etc. You would not be wondering how to tell if Jesus is coming back soon or not. You would not question whether he can come back this year or next. You would know you are safe to live your life and pursue your goals and dreams without them being interrupted by the end of the age.

Moreover, you would never fall again for another speculative or date-setting prophecy theory that many Christians end up following year after year. You wouldn't fall for these counterfeit theories because you'd already know the real answer from Jesus himself on what he said were the "signs of his coming and the end of the age" (Mt 24:2).

By the end of this article you will indeed understand Jesus' words like never before and have confidence about where we are in prophecy.

Examining Jesus' Problematic Answer on the Signs of the End

If you still think you understand Jesus' answer, you may change your mind when we see it broken down and dissected logically. Let's do that now.

Notice first that Jesus starts his answer to the disciples by giving two predictions, now fulfilled in history (H1 and H2), of what to expect before the end. He plainly says that these developments *are not signs of the end* and are therefore nothing to be alarmed about:

Matthew 24:4–6 (HCSB)—4 Then Jesus replied to them: "Watch out that no one deceives you. 5 [H1] For many will come in My name, saying, 'I am the Messiah,' and they will deceive many. 6 [H2] You are going to hear of wars and rumors of wars. See that you are not alarmed, because these things must take place, but the end is not yet. *For...*

Notice there are two predictions (labeled H1 and H2 in brackets by each one above). History clearly shows Jesus was right that deception in his name followed soon after and has continued to this day. Same with wars and rumors of wars. Nothing unique in either of these. Not signs of the end because they have been with us from the beginning and continue. Real signs of the end must be unique or unprecedented for them to be useful gauges of a special time called the "end of the age."

By the way, this statement by Jesus that "the end is not yet...For/because" contradicts the popular "imminent return of Christ" doctrine you may have been taught. That doctrine states that the reason Jesus said "no one knows the day or hour of my coming" is because it is imminent or able to come at any time without a prior prerequisite event. However, Jesus in the above verses connects his coming with the end of the age and promises to reveal signs of when the end is finally arrived.

The "for / because" introduces the next couple verses where he will finally cover these "birth pain" signs of the end of the age when his coming is possible (labeled B1 and B2). In other words, until we see what he lists next, his coming is not possible and not imminent because the end has not yet arrived.

Matthew 24:7–8 (HCSB)—7 *For* [B1] nation will rise up against nation, and kingdom against kingdom. [B2] There will be famines, and earthquakes in various places. 8 All these events are the beginning of birth pains.

Here he gives the end time signs that immediately precede his coming. But do you see the difficulty with what he said?

Firstly, the first birth pain sign (B1—nation vs. nation and kingdom vs. kingdom) is too similar to the first historic sign (H1—wars and rumors of wars). Both talk of wars. One is rumors and wars and the other is wars and wars (with no rumors mixed in). It's impossible to differentiate the two of them just from what he said alone.

Secondly, neither of these two birth pains is unique or unprecedented. As covered earlier, wars have always been with us, even before Christ. Earthquakes and famines have always happened in various places. That's the very nature of severe calamities like these. They happen in different places over time, and not, say, *every place* at once (which would be unique and, of course, *devastating!*)

The Beginning of Birth Pains?

When you carefully analyze Jesus' words like that, it's difficult to defend them. We all naturally want to rush to Jesus' defense and read his words in unconventional ways to explain how they *do* make sense. But all the attempts and approaches require stretching or torturing the words out of their plain meaning or plain context.

But there is no mistaking what he is plainly saying here. He shared what would happen before the end so his disciples would not be alarmed or confused thinking the end had come. He then pivoted into the end time signs using the word "for..." Further, when he finished with these end time signs, he labeled them "birth pains." Of course, a woman endures birth pains only when she has come to the end of her pregnancy and has begun to deliver her child. Jesus is saying that his own coming is also preceded by difficult pains.

Let's remember that in 280 days of pregnancy, a woman finally only has birth pains in the last day or two. She does not have these in the previous 278 days of her pregnancy. They are unique to the end.

For Jesus to label certain events as birth pains, they would similarly only come at the end of the 2000 year waiting period we've been in since his first coming. They could not be events that match anything over the last 2000 years. They would be unprecedented. In this way, when we finally do see them, we could know that we are finally near the end of the age and his coming.

Yet, again, wars, earthquakes and famines in various places are nothing special. Is it any wonder every generation has thought they were the *last generation?* They see a temporary increase in severity of any of these things and guess that this is what Jesus meant. But a woman's birth pains do not start as soon as she is pregnant and slowly increase over time. They come suddenly and severely and only at the end.

And by the way, contrary to claims by many trying to explain Jesus' words, earthquakes are not on the increase in this century. That's not my opinion; it's what the authorities on earthquakes say, the USGS and British GS.

Finding Jesus' Original Words Describing the End Time Signs

Then what's the answer? You'll be pleased to know Jesus is not to blame. He did not give some impenetrable, mysterious or allegorical answer that we have to torture, struggle with or speculate about. Instead it looks like a Greek scribe or translator is to blame for the difficulty of the passage.

I discovered this while reading a less popular Bible version I owned. I had bought it because, rather than relying *only* on the Greek NT texts like most popular Bible versions, it leveraged the Hebrew and Aramaic NT texts that are available. When I came across the passage in question, I was shocked at what I read there in this new version:

Matthew 24:7 (Hebrew Roots Version)—For nation will rise up against nation, and kingdom against kingdom. There will be famines, and *earthquakes in* every *place.*

[Note: you can read the entire Matthew Hebrew online for free in this Schonfield translation.]

Earthquakes in Every Place

Instead of earthquakes and famines in "diverse" or "various places," it says they would be in "*every* place."

Do you understand the difference this makes? Earthquakes and famines happening in every place at once is at last a unique sign. It's unprecedented in recorded human history and therefore could serve as a sign of something new: the end of the age.

But what could cause this? It certainly points to a global cataclysm or a violent upheaval on the planet. If you have seen your share of Hollywood disaster movies, you might already have a guess at the source.

But you don't have to guess if we look at the parallel passages to this text in Luke and later in Revelation.

LUKE ADDS TWO BIRTH PAINS THAT EXPLAIN THE CATACLYSM'S SOURCE

Luke 21:11 (HCSB)—There will be violent earthquakes, and famines and plagues [pestilences] in various places, *and there will be terrifying sights and great signs from heaven.*

According to Luke's account, Jesus also mentioned plagues to go along with the earthquakes and famines and something else that helps us identify the cause. He says there will be terrifying sights and great signs in the heavens. If you see something new in the sky getting bigger as it approaches earth, this would be terrifying because of the possibility of a collision or impact. The movie *Deep Impact* portrayed exactly such a scenario.

REVELATION'S PARALLEL TO JESUS' WORDS

Revelation parallels Jesus prophecy with greater detail. If you doubted the reliability of the minor Bible version quoted above as saying "earthquakes and famines in every place," check out what Revelation predicts in the end times beginning at the 6th seal:

Revelation 6:12–14 (HCSB)—12 Then I saw Him open the sixth seal. A *violent earthquake* occurred; the *sun turned black like sackcloth* made of goat hair; the entire *moon became like blood;* 13 the *stars of heaven fell* to the earth as a fig tree drops its unripe figs when shaken by a high wind; 14 the *sky separated like a scroll* being rolled up; and *every mountain and island was moved from its place.*

Revelation describes solar and lunar eclipses, meteor showers and the sky departing which would match the terrifying sights and signs in the heavens Jesus described. As well, we have here a violent earthquake. It must be a global earthquake in "every" place because it moves "every" mountain and island out of its original place. All this is unique and unprecedented and makes for actionable end time signs just as Jesus clearly intended to give.

The Cause?

If you want to see what happens next, read Revelation 7 and 8 up until the 4th trumpet (Rev 8:12). You will learn about the coming of:

great winds

a meteor storm burning up all the grass on earth

an asteroid impacting the ocean and destroying ships and sea life

a star or planet named Wormwood being blamed for poisoning fresh waters (think death and pestilence)

a one third reduction of all day and night light sources reaching earth's surface (think cold and famine and more pestilence)

All of this points to this new named body Wormwood coming close enough to earth to gravitationally and (to some degree) physically interfere with our planet.

Jesus' End Time Signs Understood

Very scary stuff, but I did not cover this to scare you. We were trying to understand the very practically useful answer Jesus gave for the sign that his coming was finally near.

> Now we know what it is. Jesus was predicting an end time global cataclysm brought on by something new from space, something terrifying. Also, based on his further words in Matthew 24, this all happens before the rapture and before the Great Tribulation.
>
> What this means is that until this global cataclysm comes, the end of the age has not begun and Jesus' coming is not near. No matter what theory you hear from even fellow Christians to the contrary, do not believe them. Believe the words of Jesus only. He said to look for severe global earthquakes and famine as the sign of the end of the age.
>
> "Take heed that no man deceives you" (Mt 24:4). Accept no substitute counterfeit theory that comes down the pike, no matter who says it.
>
> If you're worried about going through this, don't. Prophecy covers how God has an end time escape plan for all his servants. You will be able to take part in it when the time comes just because of the same desire to know and follow God's word that led you to find and read this article today. Again, don't worry as God has to make an escape plan that we can all qualify for no matter how little we understand of the Bible, how little we pray, how little we fast and how often we seem to fall short.[2]

Although well-researched, Tim McHyde's prophetic interpretation that the earthquakes in *diverse* places in Matthew 24 should more accurately indicate *every* place is undoubtedly terrifying. This would mean that tens of thousands of earthquakes would be occurring around the world simultaneously. Most certainly, this would be the absolute end of time. It is an interesting interpretation—and tremendous fodder for an action-packed Hollywood movie—but many are having a hard time even thinking in these cataclysmic terms.

This upsetting "end of the world" scenario just helps to underscore our Master's admonition to *be ready!*

Endnotes

1. See http://www.escapeallthesethings.com/about.htm.
2. See http://www.escapeallthesethings.com/sign-of-jesus-coming-end-age.htm.

CONCLUSION

THE BOTTOM LINE is to be ready to meet your Maker. We are reminded of the powerful, challenging scriptures found in Matthew. Please, however this book has challenged you; *think on these verses:*

> Heaven and earth will pass away, but My words shall not pass away. But of that day and hour no one knows, not even the angels of heaven, nor the Son, but the Father alone. For the coming of the Son of Man will be just like the days of Noah. For as in those days which were before the flood they were eating and drinking, they were marrying and giving in marriage, until the day that Noah entered the ark, and they did not understand until the flood came and took them all away; so shall the coming of the Son of Man be. Then there shall be two men in the field; one will be taken and one will be left. Two women will be grinding at the mill; one will be taken and one will be left.
>
> Therefore be on the alert, for you do not know which day your Lord is coming. But be sure of this, that if the head of the house had known at what time of the night the thief was coming, he would have been on the alert and would not have allowed his house to be broken into. For this reason you be ready too; for the Son of Man is coming at an hour when you do not think He will.

> Who then is the faithful and sensible slave whom his master put in charge of his household to give them their food at the proper time? Blessed is that slave whom his master finds so doing when he comes. Truly I say to you, that he will put him in charge of all his possessions. But if that evil slave says in his heart, "My master is not coming for a long time," and begins to beat his fellow slaves and eat and drink with drunkards; the master of that slave will come on a day when he does not expect him and at an hour which he does not know, and will cut him in pieces and assign him a place with the hypocrites; in that place there will be weeping and gnashing of teeth.
>
> —MATTHEW 24:35–51

We did not write this book with a "doom and gloom" purpose or with any kind of "scare tactic." But we wrote and edited this compilation of prophetic writings as an end-time victory by the believer. The Body of Christ has so much to look forward to. For those who have not accepted Christ, the end will be the end!

So let us encourage you with these exciting scriptures:

> And it shall come to pass afterward that *I will pour out My Spirit on all flesh;* your sons and your daughters shall prophesy, your old men shall dream dreams, your young men shall see visions. And also on My menservants and on My maidservants I will pour out My Spirit in those days. And *I will show wonders in the heavens and in the earth: blood and fire and pillars of smoke. The sun shall be turned into darkness, and the moon into blood,* before the coming of the great and awesome day of the LORD.

> And it shall come to pass that whoever calls on the name of the LORD shall be saved. For in Mount Zion and in Jerusalem there shall be deliverance, as the LORD has said, among the remnant whom the LORD calls.
>
> —Joel 2:28–32, NKJV

> But Peter, standing up with the eleven, raised his voice and said to them, "Men of Judea and all who dwell in Jerusalem, let this be known to you, and heed my words. For these are not drunk, as you suppose, since it is only the third hour of the day. But this is what was spoken by the prophet Joel:
>
> 'And it shall come to pass in the last days, says God, that I will pour out of My Spirit on all flesh; your sons and your daughters shall prophesy, your young men shall see visions, your old men shall dream dreams. And on My menservants and on My maidservants I will pour out My Spirit in those days; and they shall prophesy. I will show wonders in heaven above and signs in the earth beneath: blood and fire and vapor of smoke. The sun shall be turned into darkness, and the moon into blood, before the coming of the great and awesome day of the LORD. And it shall come to pass that whoever calls on the name of the LORD shall be saved.'
>
> —Acts 2:14–21, NKJV

The bottom line: Be alert! Be ready!

> Therefore be ye also ready: for in such an hour as ye think not the Son of man cometh.
>
> —Matthew 24:44, KJV

May God continue to bless you as you become more alert to God's Word, His prophets, and your surroundings. Always *be ready* for His soon return!

This is *your* victory!

AFTERWORD

ETERNAL LIFE IS obtainable to every man, woman, boy, and girl in this world, no matter who they are, where they live, or what they have done. It is freely given to any and all who will receive it. Simply learn of Jesus, the promised Messiah; invite Him into your life as Lord and believe He died on the cross for all of your sins and rose from the grave.

There is a kingdom of heaven...and a coming resurrection for both those who are going to heaven and for those who are going to hell. Learn of Jesus and believe in Him, for He was the only one who has ever loved you enough to replace you with Himself on the cross.

Jesus was crucified: He shed His blood, suffered, and died on the cross to save you from your sins and from the utter darkness, aloneness, and torment of hell.

All you have to do is to accept it, believe it, and trust in it. That is why Jesus is called Savior. He now lovingly and graciously offers you life in heaven. We have to consciously receive it and accept it in faith. Honestly acknowledge you have sinned and fully trust in Him alone to save you from your sins and from hell; then repent or turn away from those things God says are wrong and turn back to God, and you will go to heaven. With open arms, He will receive all who will come to Him in faith and in love.

This is God's promise! It is only through His grace that you go to heaven. The only unforgivable sin is to reject God's love and His free offer of eternal life in the kingdom of heaven by rejecting His Son, Jesus Christ. His purpose was not to convict the sinner, but to save the sinner from the eternal torture of hell. He lovingly and willingly shed His blood and bore all of our sins and guilt on the cross so we can be "washed clean" and forgiven of all our sins.

The Bible warns there will be no peace in our hearts or minds until we make peace with God through His Son, Jesus.

GOD'S PLAN FOR YOUR LIFE!

"What must I do to be saved?" is the cry of men and women. God's Word—the Bible—provides clear answers. You can literally be ready when the big earthquake comes—to spend eternity with Your Maker, Jesus Christ!

1. Acknowledge Your Sin

> And the publican, standing afar off, would not lift up so much as his eyes unto heaven, but smote upon his breast, saying, God be merciful to me a sinner.
>
> —LUKE 18:13, KJV

> For all have sinned, and come short of the glory of God.
>
> —ROMANS 3:23, KJV

2. Repent of Your Sin

> Repent ye therefore, and be converted, that your sins may be blotted out, when the times of refreshing shall come from the presence of the Lord.
>
> —ACTS 3:19, KJV

...except ye repent, ye shall all likewise perish.

—Luke 13:3, KJV

3. Confess Your Sin

That if thou shalt confess with thy mouth the Lord Jesus, and shalt believe in thine heart that God hath raised him from the dead, thou shalt be saved.

—Romans 10:9, KJV

If we confess our sins, he is faithful and just to forgive us our sins, and to cleanse us from all unrighteousness.

—1 John 1:9, KJV

4. Forsake the Past

Let the wicked forsake his way, and the unrighteous man his thoughts: and let him return unto the LORD, and he will have mercy upon him; and to our God, for he will abundantly pardon.

—Isaiah 55:7, KJV

5. Believe on the Lord

For God so loved the world, that he gave his only begotten Son, that whosoever believeth in him should not perish, but have everlasting life.

—John 3:16, KJV

He that believeth and is baptized shall be saved; but he that believeth not shall be damned.

—Mark 16:16, KJV

6. Receive the Gift of Eternal Life

He came unto his own, and his own received him not. But as many as received him, to them gave he power

> to become the sons of God, even to them that believe on his name.
>
> —JOHN 1:11–12, KJV

If you have not made your eternal decision, you can make it right now! It is so profound, so eternal, yet in many cases, so simple. Pray with us right now:

> *Lord Jesus, I believe You died for my sins and I ask Your forgiveness. I receive You now as my personal Savior and invite You to manage my life from this day forward. Amen.*

God wants to give you a new life of peace and victory. God wants to give you the peace that passes all human understanding. By faith, receive what God has already done for *you* today!

ABOUT THE AUTHORS

STANLEY HOERMAN WAS raised in a godly home with nine children. He learned to be a hard worker. But his father was more concerned about their spiritual development. They were good Lutherans.

At the age of nine, Stanley prayed the sinner's prayer. Instead of going to college, he joined the U. S. Marines.

Just like Jesus, Stan spent many years as a professional carpenter. Then he started to buy rental properties.

Curious, he attended some "Jesus People" meetings where he was impressed to fast for 30 days. While fasting, God overhauled Stanley's entire life. Stan read through the entire Bible. He fell in love with Jesus and was baptized in the Holy Spirit.

He taught about fasting at the local Catholic high school where he later married that teacher / nun who eventually left the convent. Stan and Rose Marie have been married for over 40 years. She started the Women's Aglow Chapter in Manhattan, Kansas, where she served for seven years on their board. Rose Marie was a state leader in Northeast Kansas with Women's Aglow for many years.

Stanley Hoerman started the Full Gospel Business Men's Fellowship International Chapter in Manhattan, Kansas, and was on the National Board of Directors for 25 years.

BOB ARMSTRONG is an ordained minister who founded Love-Link Ministries, an evangelistic and humanitarian organization, having worked in 45 countries. He has trained over 49,000 pastors and leaders in 13 different countries. Bob's father was the editor of Oral Roberts' *Abundant Life* magazine for over a decade. A graduate of Oral Roberts University (in fact, the seventh student to ever attend ORU), he is a coordinator of major print and television projects and is mainly known for his writing abilities as editor of various publications and ghost writer for scores of books. Over two million people read something that Bob writes every month. For over 12 years he was Senior Editor of the FGBMFI *Voice* magazine. He has authored numerous books, including *Razor's Edge: From Bin Laden's Home to Divine Appointments* and *Stop the Y2K Madness*, among others.

CONTACT THE AUTHORS

FOR FURTHER INFORMATION about the subject matter of this book, additional copies of this book, your comments, or for prayer, please contact:

Stanley Hoerman
Earthquake
P. O. Box 988
Manhattan, KS 66505

Or:

bobkimandb@gmail.com